SALES-FREE SELLING

The Death of Sales and the Rise of a New Methodology

By
STEVE FRETZIN

DEDICATION

I would like to dedicate this book to my son, Andrew. Though he is only six years old, my greatest hope is that he will learn the preciousness of life earlier than I did. The sparkle in his eyes and sweet smile motivate me every day to be a better father and human being.

ACKNOWLEDGMENTS

Many friends, partners, and mentors contributed to my success and ultimately the success of this book. An easy starting point is with my beautiful wife, Lisa. Her unlimited support for me in my endeavors has allowed me to pursue my dreams to their fullest.

I am grateful, also, for the support of my family, including Adam, Karen, Sharon, my father Larry, who always pushed me to be better at anything I tried. I also want to thank my mother-in-law Nancy, Sol, and, of course, GG.

Another big thank you goes to Steve Hamburg, former client and now close friend. Steve inspired me to write this book and came up with a premise that I know will be enlightening to readers.

Thanks also to Steve Amiel, Jeff Bizar, Jackie Camacho-Ruiz, Joey Davenport, Neil Dishman, Clare Fitzgerald, Mary Jane Grinstead, Michele Kelly, Scott Kempler, Joanne Levine, Lane Moyer, Brent Novoselsky, and Alan Sklar.

Finally, I would like to thank my former sales coach, Dr. Keith Winfree, who saw something special within me that led me to become a successful sales coach.

FORWARD

My name is Steve Hamburg. So you can better understand why I am writing the foreword for this book, let me provide a little background about myself and describe how Steve Fretzin changed my life. I started my first company in 2003 and then leveraged relationships I had established during my professional career to make ends meet for approximately three years.

After I completed a nine-month contract with a Fortune 10 company that originated from a very serendipitous sequence of events, I was faced with the harsh reality that I had no new contracts to deliver upon and no sales pipeline. My financial reserves were quickly becoming depleted. I was on the brink of disaster.

A colleague of mine invited me to a luncheon hosted by Steve Fretzin, who introduced me to the concept of hiring a sales coach. I quickly saw that working with a sales coach could help me turn things around for my company.

Steve and I agreed upon a seven-figure sales goal, and I entered into a contract accordingly. After the first couple of months, Steve recognized that I was not fully committing myself to his sales system. He initiated a one-on-one meeting and told me in no uncertain terms that I either needed to commit to the sales system, or we were not going to be successful. I fully committed and never looked back; five months later Steve and I hit my seven-figure sales goal.

I'm not here to impart the specific aspects of the sales system; that's what this book is going to do for you. What I will say is if it weren't for Steve coaching me, teaching me the sales system, and helping me tailor it to the industry I serve, I would not be a thriving business owner today. Additionally, Steve's sales system has helped me personally with my friends and family members. The sales system is all about listening, asking better questions, and honoring commitments, which, if applied effectively, will enable you to achieve seemingly unattainable personal and professional goals.

Prior to working with Steve, I thought that only a company's products or services could be differentiators; I never imagined that a differentiator could be the sales process itself. I've had a number of clients inform me that the sales process I had employed was unlike anything else they have ever experienced. They have commended me on my ability to listen and translate what they communicated into solutions that could resolve their issues.

Steve worked with me to internalize processes that I will carry with me for the remainder of my career. Today, five years after working with Steve, I still follow his teachings to the letter, and business has never been more profitable.

Reading, processing, and applying the sales methodologies conveyed in this book will help you be successful, too. Invest the time to read this book and take the leap of faith required to apply Sales-Free Selling. You will not be disappointed.

Good Luck!

Steve Hamburg, President of Eclipsecurity, LLC.

CONTENTS

THE CLIENTS

———

DAN

Dan Klein's thoughts wandered as he waited for the toast to pop up from the toaster. He'd mentioned to his wife, Theresa, the night before that three of his colleagues had been let go recently. They had been billing plenty of hours and had great relationships with the firm's clients, but they weren't bringing in much new business. The news had made Dan and the other lawyers at the firm very nervous.

Over the past few weeks Dan had been evaluating his own book of business, and there was definitely cause for concern. He loved practicing law, but he didn't have any training as a business developer. He certainly didn't enjoy the thought of having to develop new business and his mediocre numbers showed it. Even though there was cause for concern, Dan didn't want Theresa to worry, but he wanted her to be aware of the situation. That's why he also mentioned the sales training program he was starting today.

Dan hadn't loved the idea of taking time away from his clients and cases, but this sales coach had been highly recommended by one of the more successful partners in the firm. Dan knew he needed to take action somehow, especially considering how quickly the industry seemed to be contracting. Law firms, like everybody else, were struggling. But Dan loved being a lawyer, and he was willing to do whatever it took to stay relevant—and employed. From conversations with more established partners at the firm, he knew that the key to having control over his future would hinge on his success in developing a strong book of business. He knew he had to work harder on developing his client base. He just hoped this training program wouldn't turn out to be a waste of time.

His toast popped just as Theresa appeared in the kitchen. Their two boys, ages eight and five, bounded in as well.

"What's the schedule for the sales class?" Theresa asked as she started pouring cereal for the kids.

"Every Monday for the next several weeks," he replied through bites of toast.

"Is it only for attorneys?"

"No, I think it's going to be a small group of people from across industries."

"I thought only kids had to go to school," Dan's eight-year-old remarked.

Theresa smiled. "Adults go to school, too, sometimes," she said, waving her hand through her son's hair. "You're never too old to learn new things."

"What kind of class are you going to, Daddy?" the five-year-old asked as he climbed into his chair to join the conversation.

Dan paused to think of an easy explanation. "Well, it's a class to learn how to sell things."

"I thought you were a lawyer," the eight-your-old remarked.

"I am. And this class is going to help me sell myself as a lawyer."

"Oh," his son replied, seemingly satisfied as he turned his attention to his cereal.

"And hopefully help me keep my job," Dan muttered under his breath as he dropped his plate into the dishwasher.

"I'm off," he said, checking the clock.

"Good luck today," Theresa said, patting his arm. "Hope it goes well."

———

STACEY

Stacey Wilkinson woke up with a headache, regretting having overindulged in red wine at a late dinner with friends the night before. As she sluggishly rolled out of bed and started getting ready, she wished the sales program beginning today had a later start time. But she was glad for the break from her everyday routine and for a chance to escape the office and sales appointments for the day.

"Why do I go out on Sunday nights?" she asked her roommate Melissa as she joined her in the kitchen.

"I think the question is: Why do you go out so *late* on Sunday nights?" she laughed as she poured a cup of tea and handed it to Stacey.

Stacey eyed Melissa as she sipped the tea. "You're bright-eyed as usual," she said.

"I guess."

Melissa loved her job as a corporate accountant. Stacey hated numbers, but she was envious of Melissa for being able to work on projects in the office all day without any pressure to meet sales goals or pound the pavement looking for leads. Stacey had sort of fallen into her sales career, having lacked much direction after graduating from college with a liberal arts degree. She liked meeting and interacting with new people in her sales calls, but she'd been losing motivation over the past couple of years, and she just wasn't closing enough business for the plumbing supplies company where she worked.

"I'm starting a new sales training program today," she said, looking up to gauge Melissa's reaction. She had the feeling that all her negativity had been wearing on Melissa lately.

"Really? I thought you'd given up on those."

"I did, but this one actually sounds like it's going to be different. A sales coach is running it. Janet, that friend of mine in hotel convention sales, referred me to him, and she said he has a unique approach to sales. He made a world of difference to her. So, I'm hopeful this one will help."

"That's great," Melissa said. "What did your boss say about it?"

"He thought it was a good idea," Stacey said, gathering her papers and purse. "Are you ready to go?" she asked, changing the subject to avoid mentioning that she had to split the fee with her boss in order to get into the program.

"Yep, let's go," Melissa said, upbeat as always. "You'll have to tell me all about it tonight."

———

CHERYL

Every morning felt like a race to Cheryl Jenkins. After getting her two toddlers settled at the kitchen table with her husband Jeff, she hustled back upstairs to quickly apply blush and mascara. Stomach rumbling, she hoped there would be some muffins at the sales class she was attending this morning. She had to make a quick stop at the IT consulting firm she owned before the class started, and she knew she was cutting it close.

"Hey Jeff," she called downstairs. "What time are you going to be home tonight?"

"Uh, probably about seven."

"Ok, I'll pick up the girls tonight," she said, knowing he wouldn't be able to get to the daycare on time to pick up their daughters. "But that means I have to leave in a few minutes so I have time to stop at the office before my class today."

"What class?" he asked, entering their bedroom to pick out a tie, the toddlers trailing behind him.

She rolled her eyes. "I told you about this. I'm starting that sales program today."

He paused to think about it. "Oh, that's right."

She sighed as she fastened her earrings, annoyed that he didn't remember. She'd been having a hard time securing new business lately, and her company—and her family's bank account—was suffering.

"I really liked Scott, the sales coach, when I met him at that networking event. But this program better be good. I can't afford to waste time away from the office."

"You work so hard, honey. Don't worry," he said distractedly, watching the girls playing in the laundry basket.

"It doesn't matter if I work *hard* if I don't have anyone to work *for*," she laughed, thinking back to when she first started the company and could barely keep up with all the clients she had.

But when the economy started to tumble, her smaller clients started dropping off. At first, she was almost grateful, because it gave her more time to focus on her largest, most demanding client, a manufacturing company that had hired her for a two-phased project. The first phase had gone well, but once they entered the second phase, everyone involved realized she didn't have the capacity to meet the requirements. The company had to bring in another firm, and she hadn't devoted enough time, or any time if she was being honest, to develop a solid pipeline of potential new clients.

"Oh, you'll have new clients beating down your door in a few months," Jeff told her.

Jeff knew about her business troubles, but he always had faith that her business would succeed. She appreciated his support, but sometimes even that felt like added pressure on her. It was like he expected her to succeed just because she always had.

"Let's hope so. Can you get the girls dressed? I really have to run."

"No problem."

"Have a good day, girls," she called, starting down the stairs and smiling as she watched her pajama-clad daughters race off down the hall.

WEEK 1:
GETTING IN THE RIGHT
FRAME OF MIND

―――

Arriving at his office, Scott greeted each member of his staff before sitting down at his desk to collect his class plans for the morning. The start of a new session usually followed the same structure: introducing his clients to one another and then explaining his philosophy and process. They'd be learning from and helping each other over the next few months, and Scott knew it was important that everyone be made to feel comfortable. Before jumping into the training, Scott always wanted his clients to get to know each other and the different, or very likely similar, challenges they were facing. Their situations, backgrounds and challenges were unique, but Scott knew that the solutions for each of them would be the same.

Hearing voices in the reception area, Scott headed over to the conference room to greet his new clients.

After everyone was settled in at the round table and Scott welcomed the group, he turned to Cheryl, a petite, nicely dressed woman with a brown bob and big brown eyes.

"Hi Cheryl, nice to see you again. Please take a minute and tell everyone a little bit about yourself and what brought you here today."

"Sure. I'm Cheryl Jenkins, and I founded an IT consulting business, Acora, LLC, two years ago. I landed a big manufacturing client right out of the gate, hired two consultants, and took on business from several smaller clients as well. Things were going well at the beginning. I made sizeable investments in our website and established a series of seminars to heighten our visibility and generate leads. The work from the manufacturing client has been steady but isn't enough to carry us. The seminars didn't take off and we're struggling to find more clients. I'm at the point where I either need to find a way to breathe new life into the business or call it a day and dissolve the company."

From his previous conversations with Cheryl, Scott knew she was extremely motivated and well educated. Starting the business had been a gamble for her. She was in her thirties, had young children, and needed to stabilize the business. She had deep industry knowledge and a lot to offer her clients, but she needed more direction to build her client base and design a more detailed plan for the future. He had sensed her frustration the first time they'd talked.

Scott thanked Cheryl and moved on to Stacey, a salesperson for Blake Plumbing. Scott knew Stacey had been struggling at work, and her boss was losing patience with her poor sales performance. She had good instincts and had told him that she had read all the books and attended the key sales seminars in the area, but she was in a downward spiral. She made a quick introduction to the group.

"Hello there, my name is Stacey. I've worked in sales for Blake Plumbing for four years, and believe it or not, I actually like the plumbing supplies business," she began, tucking her long, wavy blonde hair behind her ear. "I know my products, and my company has invested a lot of time and money in me. But I'm really struggling to close new deals. I feel like I'm letting my boss down and not carrying my weight. I've been through other sales training programs, but they haven't helped. This time it needs to be different because I don't think I can last much longer at Blake."

Scott jotted down a few ideas for Stacey and then asked Dan to describe his situation at his law firm. Scott pegged Dan as a former high school linebacker. Tall and broad, Dan had an intense gaze, and Scott guessed he was a formidable adversary in any courtroom.

"I'm a lawyer, not a salesperson," explained Dan. "But my firm increasingly is expecting its attorneys to generate business, not just practice law. Three of my colleagues have been let go recently. They were billing hours and had great relationships with clients, but rumor has it they were released because they weren't bringing in new clients. I've been looking into where I stand with my firm, and my book size is relatively small. I didn't go into law to become a salesperson. They don't teach business development in law school. But with all the downsizing at firms today, this isn't a good time to be a lawyer without a strong book of business. I need to get a better handle on how to attract clients and develop a bigger book of business. From everything I had heard about Scott, he focuses on a non-salesy approach. This is one of the main reasons I chose him to help me with developing my book of business. I never want to been seen as a pandering salesperson."

Scott glanced around the room and noticed his clients nodding. He could tell they were commiserating. It was time to brighten the mood.

"I know I've talked to you all individually, but I wanted to take a moment this morning to share a few things about myself and my background before we begin. In fact, I'll go all the way back to college," he said with a smile.

"In school, I was a classic underachiever— the solid C student." Scott paused as a look of surprise crossed the faces of his new clients. "My teachers always said I had potential but lacked focus and needed to get serious. To be honest, I often felt like a failure because I didn't get good grades, and I had a hard time studying. When I entered the real world, I realized I had a knack for sales, but I wasn't anything special and I still lacked focus. I worked my way up into increasingly better positions, but I still wasn't where I wanted to be—and I knew I could do better. That's when I started working with a sales coach."

Scott wanted his clients to realize that even the coach had a coach.

"Working with a sales coach was a life-altering experience for me. It not only enhanced my sales techniques, but it also helped me realize how much I love the sales process. And most importantly, the experience got me started on a path toward true success by unlocking my potential and my passion. To make this story even more interesting, in my first six months working with my coach, I made dramatically more money than I had in my best year in sales."

Scott watched his clients' eyes widen. "I've been studying this field and perfecting the methods of how to succeed in it ever since I started working with my coach. I'm truly committed to enhancing the sales performance of my clients. I got into this business to help people, and I have seen so many clients enjoy greater success after embracing and learning my methodologies."

So they knew he was more than just talk, Scott always opened with a true success story.

"One of my favorite success stories has to do with a former client of mine named Seth. When I met Seth, his business was flailing and he wasn't sure how long he would last, but he didn't think it would be more than another three or four months. After getting to know him and his business fairly well, we recognized that his closing rate was hovering just under 20 percent—meaning that for every ten prospects he would meet, he would pick up two new clients. Based on his overhead expenses and margins, 20 percent wasn't going to keep him in business."

"Sounds like where I'm at," Cheryl mumbled under her breath.

"After about three weeks of working together, my home phone rang one night at around 9:00 p.m. It was Seth. He had just left the home of a new client, had followed my process to the best of his ability, and wanted to tell me all about it. He had just closed a new client and the light bulbs were popping everywhere for him. The next evening around 8:30 p.m., the same thing happened—Seth sharing the news of another new client. This went on for weeks, and I couldn't have been happier for Seth. His closing rate had shot up to over 85 percent, and his business was flourishing like never before. The interesting part of this story is that Seth wasn't working any harder than before. In fact, he was working less. What I'm about to tell you may come as a pleasant surprise, especially to you, Dan. There is no more selling in sales."

Scott paused to gauge the reaction of his new students before continuing. Dan was waiting expectantly. Stacey quickly looked up.

Cheryl, already paying close attention, raised her eyebrows.

"Sales, as you and I know it, is dead," Scott said. " Think about it. No one wants to be sold to, and neither do our prospects. The traditional sales model—where the salesperson tries to convince you to buy a product or service—simply isn't effective with buyers anymore. Not to mention that we all cringe at the thought of having to deal with a stereotypical salesperson. The truth of the matter is that I am not going to be teaching any of you how to sell in this program."

"Well then, you certainly have my attention, Scott," Dan commented.

"Our program is focused on the buyer's side. What I mean by that is we will be focusing on the buyer's problems, needs, and desires—not our own. This buyer-focused mentality is a major shift from the traditional sales models that you're probably used to. Focusing on our potential buyers, and listening intently to their needs, will give us the best opportunity to understand and help our new clients. Think about people's most basic needs. What are they?" Scott asked.

Cheryl jumped in first. "Food and shelter."

"Love," Stacey added.

"Ah, the romantic in the room," Scott teased. "Yes, love is another one. But the need that I am talking about is the need to be understood by others. Think about this. A man is standing on a bridge about to end his life. Is that a person who feels truly understood by others? Though this is an extreme example of someone who is not understood, it makes a good point about the importance of understanding others. We're going to focus almost all of our energy on listening, questioning, and understanding our prospects. Wait and see what happens when we do," he said with a smile. "When the focus is put on our prospects' needs, and not our own, something magical happens. We close a lot more business. So with that, let's take a quick break, and then we'll get started."

———

After everyone reassembled, Scott stood and rubbed his hands together. "Alright, everyone is here for a reason, and the faster we get moving, the sooner we can address your challenges and move you all on a path to success," he said. "I have a simple but powerful formula for success that I'll refer back to often during our time together."

Scott went to the whiteboard at the front of the room and wrote:

Over the previous twelve years, Scott had virtually perfected the formula for successful business development. Having worked with hundreds of clients, he knew from experience that their success hinged on their buy-in, commitment and belief more than anything else. If he could get people to commit to his methods and follow the right behaviors, anything was possible for them.

"Success in life and in business is all about following the right behaviors," he began to explain. "Whether it's cleaning a dirty garage, making time sensitive follow-up phone calls or planning a vacation, your behaviors directly affect your attitude. Good behaviors ensure people develop healthy attitudes, while poor behaviors create negative attitudes."

Scott introduced an example. "Think about what happens when you break a promise to someone you know," he said. "Let's say you commit to meeting your friend for a movie on a Saturday night. Then you just don't show up. How would your friend react?"

"Any of my friends would be pretty annoyed," Dan chimed in.

"Right, and in addition to it being completely unacceptable to your friend, you probably would feel badly about it as well. We don't always think about it, but breaking a promise to ourselves is no different than breaking a promise to a friend."

Scott paused to let the point sink in. "Breaking a promise to yourself beats down your attitude on a subconscious level and, over time, can destroy your internal attitude and feelings about yourself. Losing faith in yourself commonly follows. And once that happens, it's nearly impossible to be successful."

Scott saw heads nodding around the room. "On the other side of the coin," he continued, "doing the right things and displaying the right behaviors can keep you positive and optimistic. Think about it. If you commit to cleaning the garage and actually accomplish it, how do you feel? If you make the business calls that you needed to make, how do you feel? Positive behaviors will always improve your attitude, which in turn affects your belief in yourself. Not very complicated to understand, but we all have things that hold us back. That's why we need to challenge ourselves and step outside our comfort zones to be successful. After all, you never hear an amazing success story that begins with, 'she just waited until it finally happened one day.'"

Scott moved on quickly to the next part of his example.

"The most successful people typically have the same attributes: optimism, commitment and belief. But those traits aren't always easy to develop. Think about all the negativity and pessimism out there today. Fear is everywhere, which certainly doesn't help business professionals who have so much riding on their business success. In sales, so much depends on having the right attitude. Unfortunately, many of us approach sales with a negative attitude, largely because of the negative perceptions out there about sales and salespeople. We think about a slick car salesman or a pushy telemarketer. But at one point or another, everybody needs to sell something. It keeps business moving. We need to look at sales differently to be successful at it. Most importantly, we need to enjoy it."

Scott knew that when his clients first came to him, very few actually enjoyed selling. Most people didn't really understand it, either. He could tell from the faces of his new clients that they weren't any different. Scott had just the right analogy to help them better understand this.

"I've played golf for about the past twenty years," Scott continued. "But recently I really wanted to focus on improving my game, so I signed up for a one-on-one lesson with Jack, a local pro. After exchanging some pleasantries, he asked me to hit a few balls so he could take a look at my swing. One by one I slapped the balls off the pad. After about ten swings, Jack stopped me. 'You don't really enjoy swinging the club, do you Scott?'"

"I was stunned by his comment and asked him what the hell he was talking about. But Jack just smiled and said: 'Scott, I'm watching you step up to the ball and hit it, but you don't seem to be enjoying your swing. What do you think the game of golf really is?' I thought about it and realized that I was barely even thinking about the swing; I was just focused on where my ball was going to land. I didn't have the right mindset to truly enjoy the swing. I only focused on the outcome. I asked myself: If golf is a sport of repeatedly swinging a golf club, and I'm not enjoying the swing, then why am I playing golf?"

Scott noticed Cheryl tilt her head with interest.

"When I went home and thought about my lesson, I couldn't believe how closely it paralleled what I try to instill in my clients. Too often we rush through the sales process without really enjoying it. We race through meetings without really getting to know our prospects. We don't take the time to truly listen or understand their needs. Instead, we jump too quickly to the close the sale or some pointless next step. We're so busy trying to get to a conclusion in a business meeting that we miss out on the best part of sales—exercising the patience to nurture relationships and walk a buyer through a buying decision to see if there's a fit."

Tying back to his example about the golf swing, Scott posed a question to the group: "Would you all agree that in golf, a great swing typically produces a better result than a sloppy one?"

"Of course, just look at the beautiful swings of any of the golf greats," Dan answered.

"Well, Dan, the same holds true in a proper sales process. Rushing to close a sale without enjoyment or fulfillment along the way will produce a result, but it may not be the best result possible. Instead, it might generate outcomes like buyer's remorse, a short-term relationship or nonexistent referrals—just a few of the enemies of any business developer. To enjoy the swing in sales, it's crucial to develop relationships. We must take the time to gather information and understand the catalysts that will drive a more positive outcome and serve our clients' best interests. Focus your time and attention on the swing and maintain a positive attitude, and you'll land on the green every time."

Scott paused to let his example sink in before continuing. He knew most business development training programs typically educate people on a particular process. What made his coaching model different was that it focused on taking into account his clients' attitudes, behaviors and ability to apply what he taught. He worked side-by-side with his clients in order to ensure that the process he was teaching would be ingrained in their business practices forever.

"Ok, I'd like to talk about another key component of our success, which is what I call the Three Ps of successful business development," Scott said, writing on the board:

"One of the most important and neglected aspects of achieving success in developing new business is goal setting. And the first step to achieving the goals you set is to make a plan. Effectively generating more business requires a strong, yet simple plan."

Scott cited an example. "Let's say you're planning a cross-continent trip through Africa from the bottom of the continent to the top.

Without a plan for that trip, it might be your last. Imagine all the obstacles that could sabotage your journey—wild animals, rough terrain, renegade soldiers and many other threats. The same is true with your business development endeavors. Without a well conceived plan, your ability to be successful in developing new business can be a dangerous enterprise. Think about all of the obstacles you have to deal with every day—competition, a bad economy, difficult prospects that just want to get your lowest price. Right, Cheryl?" Scott nodded at Cheryl and she smiled back.

"I personally know hundreds of professionals who are barely getting by—in fact, are seemingly hanging on by a thread—with their businesses," Scott added. He wanted his clients to realize they would need to develop a rock-solid plan to get from where they were now to where they wanted to be. "When I talk about plans, I'm referring to things like goal setting, marketing planning and prospecting. These are core elements that everyone in a business producer role must tackle in order to set off in the right direction and stay on course."

Seeing that his clients were following, Scott moved on. "Alright, let's talk about the second P: the process," said Scott. "Who likes to cook?"

Dan's eyes lit up. "I love making chili for my family before football games."

Scott focused on Dan. "Do you use a recipe?"

"Of course."

"That chili probably wouldn't turn out very well without a recipe," said Scott. "Following a recipe ensures that a dish will be prepared consistently and successfully every time. Too many professionals who need to sell products or services for a living don't establish a recipe, or process. Not doing so is the equivalent of throwing the meat, beans and tomatoes in a pot and hoping they magically combine into delicious chili."

"A selling process must make the end result predictable. There is something incredibly powerful about knowing that a sale is going to close for you and why. Believe it or not, even knowing that a sale isn't going to close can be exhilarating, if you have clarity about the steps that were skipped and understand why the prospect isn't going to buy from you. It is also critical to understand what prevented you from closing the deal and ensure it never reoccurs. Having a predictable and relevant process makes everything work better. It's kind of like an assembly line. Pieces are assembled at one end, and the final product appears at the other."

Scott moved to the center of the room. "In addition to having a predictable process to follow, there is one more P that is critical to our success. It's performance improvement. Just because you have a recipe for a pot of chili doesn't necessarily make it blue ribbon-worthy chili."

Scott went back to the whiteboard and wrote:

- Is the recipe the best one available?
- Have I done anything and everything to improve it over time?

Practice doesn't cut it. We need to learn how to PRACTICE PERFECTLY.

"If the answer to one or both of those questions is no, then you aren't focusing on your performance," he said. "Think about some professions outside of the business world, like professional athletes, artists and chefs, to name just a few. These experts go through countless hours of planning, process and performance improvement to become great at their craft. Yet when it comes to business development or professional sales, many people do nothing to truly improve upon what they were originally taught."

Scott paused and waited for his clients to glance up. He wanted their full attention on the next point. "But the idea here isn't just about practice," he said. "It's about what I call *perfect practice*. Whether it's practicing the violin or practicing your sales techniques, one hour or one-hundred hours of practice isn't going to make any difference if you're not practicing the right things. In this program, I'll be coaching you on the right things to practice, because practice doesn't make perfect. *Perfect practice makes perfect*. It's an important distinction. Let's say you've been in sales for ten years, but in each of those ten years, you've done little to hone your skills. Couldn't we say you actually have one year of sales experience ten times?" he asked. "Over the course of this program, we'll talk about best practices for communicating, listening and qualifying. Regularly improving your skills in these areas will have the most dramatic effect on your sales results."

Scott returned to his chili example. "By tasting your chili after every batch and making the appropriate adjustments, that blue-ribbon winning chili is achievable. In sales, if you practice the process and learn from each experience, you'll see improvements. Over time, these improvements allow you to win new clients almost at will. And the process becomes easier and less intensive, which is what we are all striving for in the end. Having a great plan, a solid process and the ability to practice and improve your performance will allow you to achieve your goals year after year."

Scott glanced at the clock. He was wrapping up right on time.

"Ok, we're almost done for today. I'd like you all to take some time this week to really reflect on your behaviors, attitudes and beliefs. Think about what's holding you back and what you need to improve on in order to get the results you want. Review the 3 'P's—planning, process and performance—too. I want you all to have a firm understanding of those three principles because we'll refer back to them again and again over the next few months."

Scott paused as his clients took notes, waiting until they all looked up to begin again. "One last thing," he said. "I like to conclude these weekly sessions with what I call 'AHA moments' which are takeaways from the material we cover. Would anyone like to share their AHA moment from today's class?"

Cheryl responded first. "The formula showing how much our behavior, beliefs and attitudes affect our results is definitely a key takeaway for me."

"That was a big one for me too," Dan added. "I could really relate to your example about enjoying the golf swing. Hopefully, with your coaching, I'll be able to enjoy developing new business more."

Scott smiled. "We'll get there," he responded. "What about you, Stacey?"

"The three 'P's were a big takeaway for me—especially the idea about perfect practice and its impact on our performance," she said. "I've always felt like my sales should automatically improve with each year of experience, but it never occurred to me that I might not be learning and improving on the right things to really enhance my skills."

"Excellent AHA moments," Scott responded. "It sounds like everyone is taking home a lot of food for thought. I can say from experience that by developing positive habits, taking this coaching seriously, putting in the effort and correctly implementing the three 'P's methodology, your sales will dramatically increase. Remember, the three 'P's make selling predictable and put you on a path to success. Alright, everyone, have a great week and I'll see you back here next week."

WEEK 2:
PLANNING FOR SUCCESS

———

Scott arrived at his office early the following Monday for his next session with Dan, Stacey and Cheryl. As he waited for everyone to arrive, he thought about his impressions of them from the previous week. They definitely were eager to learn. He sensed Cheryl's drive and knew she'd be right there with him the whole time. Dan seemed a bit skeptical and would need to have some success in using the process before fully buying in. Stacey really wanted to improve, but she had a lot of bad habits that would need to be broken and might need more personal attention. He was reviewing his notes for the day when his assistant peeked in. "They're back," she said with a smile as she walked by his office.

"Thanks Ann," he called as he took a last gulp of coffee before heading to the conference room.

Dan, Stacey and Cheryl were seated and chatting when Scott walked into the conference room. After exchanging some weekend stories, Scott was ready to get started.

"I trust everyone found some time last week to think about behaviors and attitudes as well as the three 'P's," he said.

Everyone nodded.

"That's great," he said. "Alright, before we get into the specific steps required for successful business development, which I'll be sharing with you over the next several months, I want to spend a bit more time talking about planning. One of the most important—and often one of the most neglected—aspects of achieving success in developing new business is goal setting. Business professionals often have a big goal or objective somewhere in the back of their minds, but they don't take the time to clearly define it. In fact, a lot of times they simply wait around, thinking it will somehow get accomplished."

Cheryl laughed. "Yeah, funny how it never seems to work out that way."

"Right," Scott said, smiling. "The more effective method is to have a written plan for achieving the goal. If you don't write down your goal and how you're going to achieve it, you have very little chance of fulfilling your objective, especially if the goal is a significant one. For example, if your goal is to attend three networking events a month, you might easily accomplish that goal. However, if your goal is to double your client base in one year, that's a different story. You need to plan out a more specific strategy and write down the daily activities that will get you to where you want to be. And you need to constantly review that plan to make sure you're on track, hitting your targets along the way and making adjustments as needed. Of course, you need to work hard, be committed and believe that you can achieve the goal, as well."

Scott walked to the white board and wrote:

"Now, when setting a goal, it's critical to break down your objective into manageable pieces. We all know how easy it is to get overwhelmed when we start thinking about all we want to accomplish. So, take your goal and break it down into a list of daily actions and behaviors. If you want to lose ten pounds in three months, decide how many times you need to go to the gym each week, and then schedule the dates and times when you're going to go. Write that down, and write down how much weight you want to drop each week. The key is that you have to actually do the right behaviors, in this case getting to the gym, in order to achieve your goal. We must enter our commitments into our calendars and treat the time scheduled as if it was a high-profile prospect meeting. You wouldn't blow that off, right? Breaking apart a big goal into smaller, more manageable pieces is the only way to make it realistic and achievable."

Pointing to the board, Scott continued. "Peter Drucker, an influential management consultant, created this 'SMART' acronym in the 1950s regarding goal-setting, and it still holds true today," he said, pointing back to the board.

"You have to be 'SMART' when setting goals. Be specific about your goal and describe what precise behaviors will be linked to the rate, number, percentage or whatever you're trying to achieve.

Make sure there is a reliable system in place to measure your progress. Ask yourself whether your goal is truly achievable with a reasonable amount of effort and application. And assess whether your goal is relevant, meaning: Do the people responsible for fulfilling the goal have the necessary authority, knowledge and skill to reach the objective? Finally, to make sure the goal is time-bound, clearly define the start and finish dates."

Dan raised his hand. "I have a lot of words spinning around my head, Scott. Can you take us through an example on this?"

"Absolutely Dan. Let's say you want to achieve an additional $200,000 in new business this year. Be specific about how you're going to get there. For example, write down that you need to schedule two lunch meetings a week with existing clients to ask for referrals. Then, measure that activity. Note that it will take three hours a week, and schedule that time into your calendar. With that plan, examine what you need to achieve and whether it's reasonable. Let's say you think those meetings will produce one new client a month, which seems reasonable. Then, to assess relevancy, figure out what tools and skills will help you achieve your goal. It might be that you can track your activity through your client relationship management software or other tracking tools. Then, review your results every week, making adjustments as you go to improve efficiency and effectiveness. After doing all that, you set the deadline. You're going to be at $200,000 in new business by December 15."

Scott looked out over the group. "Does that help?"

"It does, thanks," Dan said, nodding as he made a few notes.

"I like to think of this 'SMART' method as well-rounded and balanced; a recipe for success in just about any area of your life. Put yourself in the best position possible in order to achieve your goals," Scott said.

Stacey raised her hand. "Scott, I've tried setting goals before. But it's never really worked for me."

"I hear that a lot, Stacey," Scott responded. "And usually it's because people too often set goals that are too big and too broad. For instance, they say things like, I want to make $100,000, or I have to hit X level of sales in Y months. But they don't identify what has to happen day in and day out in order to actually make that goal a reality. What we're focusing on here are the daily activities and behaviors that you have to commit to in order to achieve the goal for the day, the week, the month and for the year. Remember, by breaking your larger goal down into daily activities, you create achievable smaller goals along the way. The other important thing to remember is that by participating in this program and working with me, you're going to have accountability. As your coach, I'll be holding you accountable to your goals. So when we talk each week, we're going to be looking at your daily goals, activities and behaviors, and we're going to be making sure you're hitting them. If you're not achieving something, we're going to be talking about why not and how we are going to fix the issues. That accountability is something most people don't have. That's why people hire personal trainers or bring other coaches into their lives, like my swing coach in golf or a life or fitness coach. Accountability can really help people achieve goals at a higher level. At the end of the day, when people don't achieve a goal, it's usually because they aren't being held accountable, or the goal they've set is just too big or too broad."

Scott looked back to Stacey. "See how we'll be taking a different approach to setting goals?" he asked.

"Yeah, this approach will be very different than what I've done in the past," she conceded.

"Alright, let's briefly talk about marketing plans. To start, no one needs a fifty page, MBA-written marketing plan to be successful. Keeping it simple and easy to follow are the keys here. In my experience, the simpler we make our plans, the more likely we'll follow them. There are four major areas I would like to focus on regarding your plans."

Scott went to the board and wrote:

"We all know that with all of the competition out there, it's getting more and more difficult to drive new business. That said, there also are always areas where you can find yourself out ahead of your competition—where things aren't so crowded. But before you attack the marketplace, you need to prepare a basic marketing plan. Know where you are going to market your business and whom you are going to target. Have a firm understanding of why people will want to do business with you," Scott advised.

"The first area of focus is what's commonly referred to as SWOT analysis, which stands for your strengths and weaknesses and the market's opportunities and threats. The strengths and weaknesses are generally internal to you or your company or firm, and the opportunities and threats are external factors in the marketplace. So let's discuss this and get some examples on the table," he said, making a note on the board:

"Stacey, what would you say are some of your strengths and weaknesses?" Scott asked, turning back to the group.

"Weaknesses are easy," she laughed in response. "I'm terrible at dealing with rejection. In terms of strengths...I think I'm pretty strong when it comes to building relationships. I can usually connect with people right away."

"Great," Scott said. "Now, what about opportunities and threats?"

"Well, my marketplace is vast, so it does offer a lot of opportunity. On the flip side, though, there's also a lot of competition."

"Ok, thanks for sharing those, Stacey. It's really important to think through these factors. I'd like everyone to do this at home. Sit down and make a list for each area, and I guarantee it will help you with your overall approach to developing business."

Looking around the room, he saw everyone nod.

"Now," Scott said. "Let's move on to the next piece of our marketing plans, the differentiators. Let me ask you all something. Who knows more than one financial planner or investment advisor?"

"I know tons of them," Dan replied.

"What's the difference between them?" Scott asked.

Dan looked confused. "What do you mean the difference?"

Scott reworded the question. "What is truly unique about any of those that you know?" he asked, pausing to see if anyone would respond to his question. "It's hard to say, isn't it? The point I'm trying to make is that it's difficult to differentiate between two or three individuals that sell the same stuff, the same way."

"So what would a differentiator be for a financial planner?" Dan asked.

"Great question, Dan. What if there was a financial planner who generated three referrals a month for you? That would be pretty unique, right?"

"That would be amazing," Cheryl said, laughing. "Is this a real person you're talking about, Scott?"

"Actually, it is. He's my financial planner. He is one of a kind and different from all of the others I've met in the past ten years. But let's get back to the point for all of you, which is: What is your differentiator in the marketplace?"

"We provide the highest level of service in the industry," Cheryl said.

"Okay then, Cheryl, let's talk about that for a minute. Are any of your competitors saying the same thing about their services?"

"Yes," Cheryl replied. "But they don't actually provide it, whereas we do."

Scott paused for a second and scanned the faces of his clients. "The issue here, Cheryl, isn't what they actually do or don't do; it's what they say and what people believe. If your competition is saying 'best service in town,' and you're saying the same thing, it's probably not the best differentiator. Let me give you a litmus test to better understand whether you have a good differentiator. Ask yourself two questions: Is the statement you're making something that no one else is saying? And, do people actually care about what you are saying? For example, if Cheryl said that she had a money-back guarantee on her services, would that be a differentiator?"

Cheryl thought for a moment. "Yes, I believe that would."

"Why?" Scott asked.

"Because no one else in my industry has a guarantee like that, and I think it's probably something that people would appreciate. My concern about offering that would be dealing with freeloaders who are looking for something for nothing."

"Well, that's something we can discuss if it ever comes to fruition Cheryl," Scott responded. "The takeaway here is that if you have something that separates you from the pack, it can be leveraged to help you get in front of more people. Think about it this way: Would Domino's Pizza have grown so fast if they hadn't offered their thirty minutes-or-less delivery guarantee? At the time, no one else was doing it, and people sure do care about getting their pizzas delivered hot and fast. In some cases the differentiator might be the way you make your prospects feel; whether they feel listened to, valued and understood, or sold to and persuaded. Remember, you have to test your differentiators," Scott concluded, writing on the board to underscore his point:

Always Test Your
DIFFERENTIATORS

· Is it truly unique?
· Is it something your prospects really care about?

Scott paused to let his clients catch up on their notes before continuing. "Now, the next area of our marketing plans we'll focus on is where we work out the objective, strategies and tactics. This is my favorite part of the plan because it's where you break down your biggest goal into the daily activities that will help you reach your goals."

Turning back to the board, Scott wrote:

"I'd like everyone to copy this down on the top of a clean sheet of paper," Scott said. "Now, in one sentence write down your objective for the next 12 months."

Scott waited about 60 seconds.

"Now I'd like everyone to read their objectives aloud. Let's start with Stacey."

"I will achieve a goal of $500,000 in new business," Stacey said, then turned to Cheryl.

"I want to hit my revenue goal of $1.5 million."

"And I want to increase my book of business to $300,000," Dan said.

"Great," Scott continued. "Now what are some of your strategies for achieving these goals?"

"How about networking?" Dan asked.

"Perfect," Scott answered, "Write it down, Dan, under the heading of Strategy #1. Other strategies might include client referrals, developing strategic partners, cold calling or attending trade shows. We are looking for the more active prospecting channels—not the website leads or repeat business. We want to focus on the stuff you have to go after."

He waited a moment for the clients to fill in their own strategies in their notes.

"You should have three-to-five of these strategies going down the middle of your page. Now, on the far right side, you have the word tactic written down. This is the most important part of your plan. The tactics are the actionable steps that you intend to take in order to execute your various strategies. Failing to outline the tactics can undermine or really limit your effectiveness in achieving the strategies you've chosen," Scott explained.

"Dan, you mentioned networking as a strategy for building your practice. Can you think of an example of a specific tactic for being a successful networker?"

Dan thought for a moment. "How about finding good places to meet new people?"

"Great start," Scott answered. "Now ask yourself the following questions to help break the tactic down into more detail. Who are you targeting? Where can you find these people? Why are they good people to go after? When are you going to research this?"

"And all of those answers go into my tactics?" Dan questioned.

"Exactly," Scott said. "It's really critical to be as specific as possible to ensure that you know exactly how you're going to achieve success with that tactic. Break it down into two-to-four sentences that explain the 'what', 'who', 'why', 'where', 'how' and 'when'. Once you have a descriptive and actionable list of five to seven tactics for each strategy, you will be in business. All we are really doing here is going from a micro-level to a macro-level of planning. If the tactics work, your strategies will be achieved. If the strategies are achieved, the objective will be met. Meanwhile, we want to track all of this to ensure we make adjustments along the way. The last thing you want is to stay with a strategy too long that isn't working. Either make adjustments to improve the strategy or simply give up on a strategy that isn't getting results. It is critical to have enough strategies to ensure that if one fails, others will still be workable for you"

"Any questions?" Scott asked the group. Everyone seemed to be on board, so he continued.

"Since we are talking about tracking and making adjustments, I think the timing is perfect to discuss the last part of our marketing plans—your success journals. There's an old saying: 'If you can't measure it, you can't manage it.' Has anyone heard this before?"

"I have," Stacey commented.

"Great, what was it in reference to, Stacey?"

"It was something I heard at a time management seminar I attended years ago," she said.

"Well, that makes sense, because your ability to understand your numbers will be critical to improving your efforts as a producer. Sports provide great examples of this. A baseball player with a .300 batting average is likely getting paid big bucks. What about a player hitting under

.200? He's probably getting ready to be shipped down to the minors. If you were that player hitting under .200, what would you do to keep your position on the team?"

Dan responded first. "I would talk to the batting coach to figure some things out."

"Exactly," Scott said enthusiastically. "In the world of professional sports, it's all about knowing the score, timing, averages and so on. Without that information, it's very difficult to know what's not working and how to fix it. I've always found it interesting that the same principles are not used by business developers. And to be honest, for the first ten years of my sales career, I never used any type of tracking tools to improve my performance. Until the idea of tracking was introduced to me, I was like a hamster on a wheel just making the same mistakes year after year."

"It makes perfect sense though," Dan added. "I never know what's working or not. I just do what I've done based on the little I know."

"Well, we are going to put an end to that today, Dan," Scott said. "Moving forward, each of you is going to have a success journal, which will accomplish two important things. First, it will be used as a way to track your activity levels, thereby making sure they are high enough to achieve the end goal that you have established for yourself.

Secondly, it will greatly improve your conversion rates, because it will help us identify where you are struggling. For example, let's say that Stacey is getting tons of appointments, but none of them are converting to proposals. We would want to focus on her sales process with in her appointments. Or, for instance, Cheryl might be making ten calls a day but getting very few appointments. By tracking these conversion ratios, Cheryl will have a clear understanding of what's working and what's holding her back."

"Let me give you a perfect example of this. Years ago, I had a client who was seeing a lot of prospects but getting very few closes. We weren't really sure why until we started tracking his appointments in his success journal. The biggest gap we observed was that the engagement ended after the first meeting. He was only closing 10 percent of prospects. After dissecting his situation, we found out exactly why the ratio was so low. He was consistently meeting with the wrong decision makers and losing one opportunity after the next. Once we learned this, fixing it was a breeze, and my client's closing rate shot up to over 80 percent. Without tracking and measuring activities, it can be very difficult to see exactly where the gaps are in someone's process.

"The success journal will work in tandem with your objectives, strategies and tactics that we are working on together. Essentially, you are going to break down goals for yourself that will be tracked on a daily basis. Let's start by looking at one element of your strategies, say networking, for instance. What are the different elements that would allow us to know whether networking was working for us?" Scott asked.

"How about the number of events you are attending monthly," Cheryl said.

"Or the number of people you interact with at the events," Dan added.

"Both are useful for us in tracking our networking success," Scott concluded. "The various areas to track might be different from person to person. We could look at the number of events, the number of quality people you met, the number of people that met you for coffee after the event and the number of referrals you pulled out of those meetings. You should be setting goals for each of these strategies and then tracking your progress."

"But wait, Scott, how do I know what to set as my goals if I have no idea what the ratios currently are?" Stacey asked.

"Great question, Stacey. Unfortunately, this is not an exact science when starting your journals for the first time. You have to think back to your activity in the last month or two and 'guesstimate' what you think the activity was. Be realistic and work backwards from the results you've previously achieved. For example, if you know that you closed two deals from networking last month, think about how many meetings it took to get those two deals. Then go back further to how many meetings it took to get the referrals and how many events you attended. Again, not an exact science, but we do need a starting point. Do this for the two to four strategies that you identified in your marketing plan and then just break it down as you see here on the board."

Journaling/Tracking

strategy	goals	actions
networking	3 events 9 contacts 6 appointments 2 new clients	1 - 30 days of the month
client referrals	5 client meetings 4 referrals 2 appointments 1 new client	

"So now that you see how important tracking can be, I just want to reiterate the importance of keeping your activity levels high. Setting goals and developing a marketing plan are important, but those actions can be almost meaningless without your ability to execute on them. Again, what I mean by activity is how, and the degree to which, you are actively pursuing your goal. The more active you are, the more opportunity you have to practice, learn and improve every day. Baseball provides another good analogy here. Every time a baseball player has a chance to step up and swing the bat, he has an opportunity to improve his swing. The more swings he takes, the better he'll be at hitting the ball, especially if he has an insightful coach helping out. The same holds true for us: If you learn the business development process that I'll be sharing with you in these classes, but you don't get in front of enough prospects, then you won't have enough opportunities to really implement the process. The more opportunities you create, the more chances you'll have to fail, learn and ultimately improve—and the better you'll get over time."

"Scott, can I interrupt you?" Cheryl asked. "How much activity is considered enough?"

"It depends on your goals, Cheryl. This is another area where breaking down your goal into smaller, less intimidating chunks is useful. For example, let's go back to the goal of adding $200,000 in new business in one year," Scott said, drawing another chart:

If your average contract is $15,000, then you have to close about 13 new contracts to achieve that goal. In 12 months, that's at least one contract per month. Let's break that down even further. How many appointments are needed to produce one new contract? Let's say three appointments per month. Then how many people need to be contacted to get those three appointments each month?

Let's define a contact as a conversation with someone who can make a decision to buy from you. Now, we can estimate about ten contacts a month, which probably requires at least thirty minutes of calling time each week. Put all that together and you have the beginning of a prospecting plan—based on manageable and realistic numbers. Do the activity and achieve the goal. Fall behind, and you'll be playing catch up each month."

"I feel like I'm always playing catch up," said Stacey. "It seems like an endless cycle."

"You're not alone, Stacey. That's so common," Scott said, nodding. "You really need to commit to allocating the time for making the calls, going on appointments and following up with new and existing clients. My advice is to focus on balancing it out so you don't end up on a roller coaster ride from week to week."

Scott waved his hand in the air, up and down like the waves on the ocean. "One of the greatest challenges in building a predictable pipeline is to always be prospecting, even when you're busy. The rollercoaster ride is great when you're at the peak and business is streaming in. And that's when we forget or ignore our prospecting activities because we are busy with all of this new business. That's a big mistake! We need to be prospecting all the time in order to ensure our pipeline is never dry. Doing so will limit the big dips and allow you to keep driving your business forward."

"That's easier said than done a lot of times," said Dan. "So much can get in the way."

"True. Things often come up, and it can be difficult to juggle everyday responsibilities with business development goals," Scott conceded as he walked back to the table to sit with his students.

"But there's a bigger obstacle to prospecting for new business, and it's the one that really holds us back: Fear. But overcoming your fears about making calls, being rejected and hearing the word 'no' is critical to being successful. So how do we become fearless in our prospecting activities?" Scott asked. "First, you have to understand that fear in the business development arena is always self created. It's like the monster hiding under the bed. Our imaginations create all kinds of crazy scenarios that keep us from moving forward confidently. We're so afraid of 'losing' a contract that we become immobilized. But it's important to think of it this way: How can you lose something you don't already have? You can't, and you just need to consciously recognize that your fear is really a figment of your imagination. Let me pose a question: How many of you are afraid to hear the word 'no'?"

Dan and Stacey sheepishly raised their hands, and Cheryl nodded. "I am," she said. "I'm always worried things won't work out, and then I take it personally when it doesn't."

"Here's a tip: Put an end to the idea you have in your mind that everyone is going to do business with you," Scott said. "You simply can't take it personally if someone says no. A lot of times, prospects probably like you and your service but don't have a need for it at the time. So just say the word 'next' and move down the list. Even better, understand the numbers. For example, if you meet ten people at a networking event and only get two appointments, those are still two more appointments than you would have had if you hadn't attended. In the end, business development is a numbers game. You need numbers, and then you need to invest your time doing the right things with the right people."

Scott smiled as he wrapped up his explanation. "Be glad to get the no's; don't be afraid of them. Hearing a 'no' can be the second best thing that anyone can tell you because it allows you to move on. Now, I'm not suggesting that we shouldn't be persistent or try to understand why a prospect is saying 'no.' At the end of the day, if we move someone to a 'no' and get on to the next person; we save a lot of time. And time, ladies and gentlemen, being efficient with your time is the name of the game. Time is our most precious asset and needs to be respected. In the past, I used to chase after prospects for as long as a year, if you can believe it. I would travel across the country, meeting five, six or even seven times to try to convince someone to buy my services. In the time I spent chasing after one wishy-washy lead, I could easily have made a lot more sales. I had to learn how to let them go and move on to the next more qualified prospective client."

"Let's take a deeper dive into this for a minute," Scott continued. "We all know about sales pipelines, right?"

The group acknowledged affirmatively.

"When I was coming up in sales, having a full pipeline of prospective clients was critical to impress my boss and show him my value. The problem I had was in actually closing most of these deals. Many of them were just not qualified to do business with me at the time. Though they never told me why, I now understand there were countless reasons why they didn't move forward with me. Not having enough urgency, money or the fact that I was presenting solutions to the wrong person, just to name a few. To me, I just forged through without a thought or concern about the crazy amount of time I was wasting chasing after the wrong prospects. If someone didn't buy from me today, I would just move them into next month's pipeline and chase after them some more. If you think about what it means to have all of those 'maybes', 'think about its' and 'I'll get back to yous' piling up, it can really sap your time away, not to mention the emotional energy invested in those opportunities while they sit in limbo. Learning to properly qualify your prospects and move the wrong ones to a 'no' will change your life. It did for me and I no longer wonder who will buy or not, believe it or not, I actually know."

Scott studied the faces of his clients and saw that they were all truly intrigued by his revelations.

Knowing he had covered a lot of material for one day, Scott started wrapping up. "Alright, you've already started writing down some of your objectives, strategies and tactics, and I'd like you to spend some time solidifying those this week. Think more about your strengths, weaknesses and differentiators, too. And find a good place to start your success journal, whether it's in a notebook or on your computer. Now, let's hear your AHA moments before we end to-day's session. Cheryl, let's start with you."

"I'm going to be more specific in my goal-set-ting, rather than just saying I want to grow," she said. "I'm going to identify by how much I want to grow and actually figure out how I'm going to do so."

"That's great to hear," Scott said.

"I'm going to be more diligent about writing down my marketing tactics and strategies," Dan added. "And I'm going to force myself to track my activities, set up my plan to focus on the lowest hanging fruit possible and schedule time to make calls weekly to keep my activity consistent."

"Me too," Stacey agreed. "I'm actually look-ing forward to starting my success journal. I think it will keep me much more organized and on track. And putting more thought into my strengths, weaknesses, opportunities and po-tential threats will help me focus on the right targets."

"I guarantee it will," Scott responded. "Ev-eryone mentioned great takeaways. Remember, make your goals specific, measurable, achievable and relevant, and set deadlines for meeting your goals. Identify your strengths and weaknesses as well as opportunities and the threats you face. Develop strategies for meeting your objectives and follow through on the tactics necessary to achieve your goals. Keep your activity levels high and track your progress. All of the planning and actions we discussed today will put you on the right track for successful business development. Have a great weekend everyone"

WEEK 3:
BUILDING A STRONG FOUNDATION

Cheryl and Stacey arrived first to class the following week.

"So what do you think so far?" Cheryl asked Stacey as they waited for Dan and Scott.

"I'm hopeful," Stacey replied. "A friend of mine in hotel convention sales referred me to Scott. She said his coaching program was a life changer for her. She knows the ups and downs of a career in sales, but she has been on a really solid, successful path for several years now. Anyway, she knows how many seminars I've sat through in the past, how many books I've read, and she promised my time with Scott would be completely different. How did you meet him?"

"We met at a networking function for Chicago business owners. It was right after I started my business; before things got tough. We started talking about some of the things that make selling difficult today—increased competition, customer access to unlimited information and buyers who are more equipped to call the shots."

Cheryl thought back to how Scott had said that traditional selling models were becoming obsolete. "Scott described how the selling process has changed," she recounted to Stacey. "He said that most people overlook or underestimate the changes in buying behavior that have been occurring over the past five-to-ten years. He explained that there's a new relationship between buyers and sellers. Buyers are better informed and more risk adverse, and they have access to more options than ever. Selling anything in that environment requires a lot more than simply having a good product. At the time, I thought he had great points and a strong passion for his craft. But I also thought I had more than enough business at the time, and I wouldn't have to worry much about the sales process."

Cheryl remembered how things at Acora—and her confidence—started going downhill not long after that conversation with Scott. Scott's explanation of how quickly people can lose faith in themselves hit home. She turned her attention back to Stacey.

"Anyway, my company started struggling to find new clients and close deals. I realized I needed to focus a lot more on sales, and I thought of Scott and the conversation we had that night. So I gave him a call," she said, glancing up as Dan walked in.

"Good morning, Cheryl, Stacey." Dan stepped into the conference room. "My train was a bit delayed. Mind if I ask what you're talking about?"

"We were just talking about how we connected with Scott. How did you find him?" Cheryl asked as Dan settled in at the table.

"I belong to an association of attorneys, and Scott has worked with a lot of the members," he responded. "The president of the organization highly recommended Scott. I have to admit, I haven't been able to summon much motivation on this sales stuff, but in the legal field today, having control over your future all depends on the book of business you develop."

Scott walked in and turned to shut the door, smiling to himself when he overheard Dan's comment. He wanted his clients to realize that he was giving them the tools they'd need to have that control over their futures.

"We came back," Dan joked as everyone gathered around the table again.

Scott laughed. "That's always a good sign. How did the homework go for everyone last week?" he asked. "Did you make progress with your marketing plans, SWOT analysis and journaling?"

Everyone nodded.

"Great. We'll be going over your specific goals individually in our one-on-one sessions. Remember, carving out time each week to spend on these homework assignments will really help you follow along and apply this process to your own sales efforts. Now, the next topic we're going to be discussing is what really lays the foundation for successful business development."

"We're ready," Cheryl said.

Scott smiled; he could tell the group was getting comfortable and feeling positive. It was his job to make sure they stayed focused and maintained those positive attitudes.

"Earlier we talked about how sales professionals who are only focused on closing sales may be missing out on the best part about sales—developing relationships," Scott began. "Not only do I think that developing relationships is the best part of the sales process, it's also the most important, because the relationships we cultivate are the foundation for our future success in the selling process and beyond. And that's why we need to be thinking about the relationship we're developing from our very first interactions with a potential client. Success in the first ten seconds can lead you to the next five minutes or fifty minutes. In those first few seconds, either you are laying the groundwork for a strong relationship by building trust and finding commonalities, or you are losing your prospect's attention and interest."

Scott popped up, quickly moved to the whiteboard and wrote:

1. Preparation
2. Looking the part
3. Using your head
4. Finding natural affinities

"These are the four major elements for building strong relationships," he said. "So let's start with number one—preparation. Salespeople used to think the best way to build rapport at the start of a meeting was to comment on an object in the prospect's office. Something like, 'That's a beautiful fish on your wall. Did you catch it yourself?' But what do you think turns people off about that?" Scott asked the group.

"The person probably has heard the same compliment over and over," Cheryl responded.

"It comes across as fake interest," Stacey added.

"Exactly," Scott said. "You're immediately bringing to mind the image of a cheesy—and sleazy—used copier salesman. It's a lazy open. Instead, start the meeting with a well thought out comment or question that shows the prospect that you took the time to get to know him and his business. And to do that, preparation is the key. Before you even enter a prospect's office or call for an appointment, you need to gather data. Use the multitude of tools at our fingertips today: Google the person, see who he's connected to on LinkedIn, look over his tweets, research his industry or search for articles he's written. Then, when you walk in to meet him, bring along the article you found and ask him a question about it. Speak intelligently about his world and you'll immediately create likeability and trust with your new prospect."

Scott noticed his clients nodding in agreement and moved on. "Alright, I think we can touch briefly on number two: looking the part. How many times have we all sat in front of a salesperson, trying to concentrate on what he's saying, when all we can think about is his wrinkled shirt and disheveled hair?" he asked. "Even if the salesperson has a product or service that I need and is speaking quite intelligently about it, I'm going to tune him out. To build a strong relationship, you have to look, smell and dress like a professional. I always advise my clients to mirror the prospect's attire or go one step up. Cheryl, if you're going in to meet a CEO of a $20 million company at his office, what would you wear?"

Cheryl was quick to respond, "I would definitely wear a suit to that type of meeting."

"Okay, great, how about an IT director at a manufacturing business?"

"I might step it down one notch, because most IT directors don't wear suits. Especially at a manufacturing company," she replied.

"Terrific," Scott praised. "But no ripped up jeans and flip flops," Scott joked, winking as his clients smiled.

"So now that we're prepared, properly outfitted and ready to go, the next element is really important," Scott said, pointing to the third item on the board. "What I mean by 'using your head' is to really try to understand how your prospect thinks and behaves."

Dan's hand went up. "That sounds like you're telling us to read our prospects' minds."

"Not quite," Scott responded. "But what I'm talking about is easier than it sounds. Because by understanding a few basics about human behavior, we quickly can determine how to communicate more effectively with our prospects, and thus build stronger relationships. By observing how people speak and behave, and then mirroring their body language and speech patterns, you can build rapport in a very subtle manner. People typically fall into one of four different behavior styles. Have any of you ever heard of DISC assessments before?"

When Stacey nodded, Scott asked: "Have you ever taken one before, Stacey?"

"I did," she replied. "It was a few years ago, but I remember it being really accurate about me."

"DISC assessments are known to be about 90 percent accurate and can tell us a great deal about how we behave and how we like to be communicated to," Scott explained. "They also do a great job of teaching us how best to communicate with others. I'm sure you've all heard the saying, 'Treat people the way you want to be treated yourself.' Well, when we're building relationships, we should treat others the way *they* want to be treated. It's an incredibly simple but effective idea. The people we meet are all different, and therefore we should communicate with them differently based on their particular behavior style."

Scott noticed a few more elbows on the table than moments before. It was always a good sign to see his students leaning in with heightened interest.

"As I mentioned, people generally fall into one of four specific behavior styles: Dominant, Influencing, Steadiness or Compliant (DISC). Though many people have characteristics of more than one style, we can make observations about people upon meeting them that provide clues about their strongest style. Based on those observations, we can alter the way we address them and handle the conversation."

Scott turned to the board to draw a diagram:

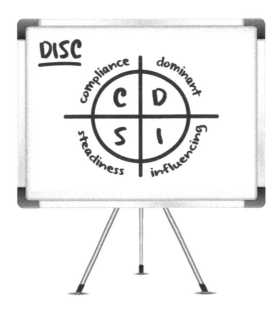

"Let's start with the dominant style. How would you describe someone who has a dominant behavior style?"

Dan jumped in first. "I deal with dominant people all the time. They're usually demanding and difficult, and rarely do they want to engage in small talk with me."

"Yes, those traits are on target. What else?" Scott asked.

"Results-focused, big-picture types, like a CEO," Cheryl added.

"Also good attributes, Cheryl," Scott said. "You are all correct, although people can fall into the high D behavior style to varying degrees—from moderate to through the roof. The key to finding out if someone is a high D is to ask questions. Then, really listen to how they answer your questions or communicate with you. For example, if they appear to be egocentric and demanding, they're likely on the high end. Characteristics such as being strong willed, forceful and determined, may put them in the middle. Decisive, competitive people often fall on the low end. Can anyone name a few famous people who fall into the high D quadrant?"

Dan thought of one almost immediately. "How about Bobby Knight?"

"That's a perfect example," Scott responded. "For those of you who don't remember Bobby Knight, he was the former basketball coach at Indiana University. His claim to fame was throwing a chair onto the basketball court during a game after a bad call. Not to mention being one of the most winning coaches in NCAA history. This guy exemplified a high 'D' behavior with his strong temper and the drive to win at any cost."

"Let's move on to the high 'I' behavior. The 'I' here stands for Influencer. These people are typically extroverted and value new experiences. They enjoy people and love to talk and share stories. Although high 'I's' often are found in sales roles, they sometimes struggle with rejection because they want everyone to like them. As a high 'I' myself, I used to avoid confrontation or speaking with prospects that might tell me 'no.' One time I even went to the movies during a work day to avoid a call I knew I'd be getting from a prospect who wasn't going to buy from me."

"Now that sounds like me," Stacey interjected enthusiastically. "I hate hearing no's from prospects, and I know I take it way too personally."

"Exactly, I'm with you on that Stacey," Scott said. "We just want everyone to love us and give us a hug, right?"

Stacey smiled and Scott continued.

"Specific descriptors for the high 'I' would include things like inspiring and magnetic on the high end, enthusiastic and convincing in the middle and trusting and sociable on the lower side. I usually think of actors and some politicians when I think about the high 'I's.' Bill Clinton and Robin Williams are good examples. Before we move on, any questions about the high 'I' or high 'D' behaviors?"

Scott's clients shook their heads.

"Let's move around the circle to the high 'S' behavior, which stands for steadiness. These are people who rely on being slow and steady to win the race, which means you just can't rush a high 'S' into something. They're often relaxed and resistant to change on the high end, passive and possessive in the middle and steady and stable on the lower end. I always think of the sixth man on the basketball team to illustrate this personality. He really doesn't care about the spotlight, but he loves being part of and supporting the team. A good example of the high 'S' for me is my wife, Laura. She constantly urges me to slow down, which usually allows me to make safer and more informed decisions. When someone comes to our door selling something, I have my checkbook out in minutes. But she will ask more questions and uncover whether we really need the product or service right now. Let me ask you all a question relating to sales. How does selling to a high 'S' affect your ability to close quickly?"

Dan stepped up first with a response. "Obviously, they are going to take a longer amount of time to research you or your offering before making a final decision. Sounds like an office manager or someone in a COO-type position might be a high 'S.'"

"Very perceptive," Scott said. "If you can uncover someone's behavior style during your opening meeting with him, how would that benefit you as the business developer?"

"That would really help us better understand how to sell to them or communicate with them, right?" Cheryl added.

"I think I get a lot of high 'D's in dealing with CEOs and presidents of companies," Dan said.

"You are all catching on very fast, and I promise to show you how this will help you to improve your communications; however, we have one more behavior to cover—the high 'C.' Now, high 'C's are very compliant by nature. This means that they are focused on the details and processes more than anything else. They might be evasive and worry-prone on the high end, exacting and neat in the middle and tactful and balanced on the lower end. Selling to a high 'C' can be complicated, because they are so risk adverse and cautious. A good example of this would be Al Gore, the former Vice President. He was always focused on facts and was very tactical in his approach to politics and the environment. There are probably a lot of accountants, CFOs and engineers that fall into the high 'C' group as well."

"So, how does this help us in our relationship building and selling?" Scott asked the group rhetorically. "It's simple. Let's go back to the old saying: treat people the way you want to be treated. Now it's treat people the way *they* want to be treated. You actually need to adapt or alter how you communicate with your prospective clients. Think about this. Do you really want to go into great detail with a high 'D' person? Conversely, does it make sense to talk about big-picture solutions with a detail oriented 'C'? Of course not. So here is a fairly reliable shortcut to help you assess your prospective client, or anyone really, without them having to actually take the DISC test."

Scott added a few words to his diagram on the board.

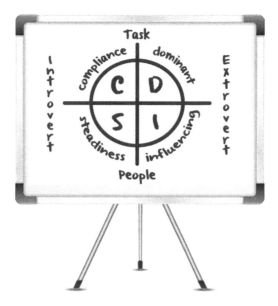

"First of all, ask your new prospective client a few questions. Get him talking about his business, family, golf trip or whatever. Then, quickly analyze the speech patterns, body language and overall demeanor. Ask yourself, extrovert or introvert? If he's a little more reserved, less chatty and closed in his body posture, he's probably introverted and more likely to be a high 'S' or 'C.' On the other hand, if he's super chatty, more animated, and open in his body language, this person might be more of a high 'I' or 'D.' If you can get that far, you're already ahead of the curve. If nothing else, you will know that this person may be a little faster or slower in making a decision to buy from you. Please keep in mind that this is not a perfect science, just a better way of assessing a situation," Scott said, pausing to let his clients catch up.

"Once you've confirmed in your mind that the person is on one side or another, try to gather even more clues about him. Ask yourself if your prospect is more people-focused or more task-focused. If the person is more task focused, he's probably more of a high 'C' or 'D.' If he's more people focused, then the 'S' or 'I' would make more sense. As an example, if your prospect is extroverted and task focused, he's more likely to be a high 'D,' like the people with whom Dan's often meeting. Or, if the person is introverted and people oriented, he's more likely to be a high 'S.' The main point here is that we need to be the chameleon and alter how we interact and communicate with prospects in order to develop the strongest rapport possible. People like people who are like themselves. I mean, think about your best friends. They're probably a lot like you. So keep in mind that if you meet someone who is introverted and task focused, and that is clearly not your style, keep a little distance between you and him. Try to break things down into more detail than usual and say things like: 'Let's follow a proven process shall we?' or 'Let's put these pieces of the puzzle back together,' because then you are speaking the language of the high 'C.' Now, let me ask: What would you say to a prospect whom you believed to be a high 'I' for example?"

Cheryl took a stab at answering. "I would try to use phrases that appeal to big-picture people, like 'let's do this together' or 'what a great experience this will be.'"

"Terrific," Scott said enthusiastically. "I think you all have the right idea now, and we'll be spending more time on these ideas over the next few months to really improve your relationship-building skills."

"Before you go on, I have a quick question," Dan said.

"Shoot," Scott said eagerly anticipating Dan's question.

"I'm just wondering why I have to adapt to be like my prospective client. Why can't I just be me?"

"You definitely want to be you, Dan. I'm not suggesting for a moment that you change who you are. But I want you to think about how someone might respond to you if they possess a completely different type of behavior style than yours. If you're communicating with your prospects in an inefficient manner, it might take you longer to build trust or likeability, or you might simply rub them the wrong way. Remember, people communicate differently and take in information differently. So, again, if you're a high 'D' and you have a very dominant, straightforward style, and you're communicating with someone who's a high 'C' and is a very analytical and detail-oriented person, you could lose him in the first five minutes of your meeting. I understand you want to be yourself, and I get that, but at the same time, you're not going to be communicating very effectively with your prospect if you don't adjust your style. So, you have to be willing to adapt and be a little bit of a chameleon in order to communicate well with the people that you're dealing with. Does that help explain my point a bit further?"

Dan looked introspective. "Yes, I see what you're saying. I don't have to hide who I am, but I may need to alter my style a bit when conversing with some prospects."

"Great, now that we have a good idea of how to communicate better and be 'like' your prospects, let's move on to the last key to driving successful relationships—what I call building natural affinities. Usually it only takes some background work and a few good questions to find the commonalities that provide a link between you and your prospect. Let's say you find out that your prospect was in the military and that you also served in the military. Or perhaps you're both parents of toddlers. Natural bonds or affinities like that can go a long way toward building trust."

Scott opened the discussion to the group. "What do you think are some good questions for uncovering commonalities?"

"I like to ask people how they got started in their businesses," Cheryl suggested.

"That's a good one," Scott said. "What else?"

"What about something like: 'Do you live nearby?'" Stacey asked. "Is that too personal?"

"Not at all, Stacey, that's a good question," Scott answered. "By starting with that and asking a few follow-up questions, you can get a feel for whether your prospect has a family, for example, or you may even discover that you live close to one another and go to the same restaurants, or you might even know some of the same people."

Dan added an idea. "If you find something you have in common in your preparation research, you could ask him about that. If I know a prospect is a golfer, I might ask him where he plays."

Scott nodded. "Those are all great examples. As you can see, if you put a little thought into it ahead of time, you can build trust and rapport very early in the process."

"Scott, I like to think that I'm pretty good at building rapport. If it comes pretty naturally to me, can I wing that part of it?" Cheryl asked.

"You know, Cheryl, even people with the best rapport-building abilities should still have a plan. You can always use your charm and personality to your advantage, but have a back-up plan, too. Do your research, go over your process and prepare questions ahead of time. Investing that time will only help you—whether rapport building comes naturally to you or not."

Scott pointed to the four elements written on the board. "These four components are the keys to building great relationships. Without building trust from the very beginning, it will be very difficult to ask more probing questions later. Remember, some things never change: people buy from people they like and trust. As you come into contact with colleagues, friends, prospects, family members, or whomever this week, I want you to think back to the 'DISC' traits we just addressed, and try to evaluate their style. Maybe even try to adjust how you're communicating with them. Maybe you'll even get along better with your co-workers and the tougher people in your families," Scott laughed.

"I'll start with AHA moments today," Stacey offered.

"How'd you know I was going to ask?" Scott joked, amused that his clients were picking up on his drill.

"I'm going to think about sales in terms of relationships more. Before, I had never really thought about building relationships with my prospects. Going on sales calls was just a chore. But thinking about prospect meetings as a chance to build relationships and trust is going to help me enjoy it more."

"Me too," Cheryl said. "I've always liked the personal interaction that comes with sales, but now I'm going to be entering meetings with more of a plan, so I can turn those connections into real relationships and build trust with my prospects."

"I'm going to keep those 'DISC' elements in mind when I'm in meetings and watch my prospects' speech patterns and body language more closely," Dan added. "And I'm going to work on adjusting my style to communicate better with prospects. As you said, people like people who are like themselves."

"I'm really glad everyone has taken these lessons to heart today," Scott said. "Building relationships is one of the most fun yet vital parts about sales. Learning about people and understanding what makes them tick can be incredibly rewarding if you just plan ahead a little better. A few weeks ago, we talked about enjoying the sales process, and I think you'll see that building relationships are a big part of that enjoyment."

WEEK 4:
SETTING STRONG AGENDAS

———

The next week, Scott entered the conference room on Monday morning to hear his clients joking about Dan being a high 'D' and Cheryl a perfect high 'S.' He smiled, as he was very pleased they were already applying the material.

"Good morning, everyone," he began. "Last week we went over relationships and the 'DISC' assessments. I asked you to think about the 'DISC' traits I outlined and try to apply them to the people you came in contact with—prospects, family members, colleagues, etc. Does anyone have any stories to share about evaluating someone's behavioral profile?"

Dan caught Scott's attention. "When I started profiling people in my office, I realized that the 'DISC' assessment is really spot-on. Once you start picking up on some of those behavioral clues, it's pretty easy to tell what quadrant people fall into. And when I started identifying my colleagues' behavior styles, I immediately started thinking of ways I could better communicate with them."

Cheryl nodded in agreement. "I had a prospective client meeting this week, and one of the first things I noticed was that the prospect wasn't making great eye contact. He seemed very introverted, so I tried to slow down my speech and give him more details. I spent more time trying to get him to open up to me, and it actually worked. We developed a good rapport. I think I would have missed an opportunity to build that relationship if I hadn't thought about the best way to communicate with him."

"That's great. I'm glad you were able to see what a difference it makes. Ok, let's switch gears," Scott said as he placed a cooking magazine on the table and opened to a page picturing a beautiful Thanksgiving dinner table.

"One of the biggest challenges for business developers is to figure out how to control their meetings with new prospects," he began. "Our prospects are always looking for quick answers and to find out our prices or rates immediately after we've just walked through the door. The truth is that we all do this. Think about the last time you updated or remodeled something in your home. Didn't you get multiple quotes and look for some free consulting along the way? We're all afraid of overpaying, so we make sales-people jump through hoops to give us information and pricing."

Stacey looked up. "I definitely have that problem," she said. "I get so flustered by all the questions that I can't really control the flow of the meeting."

"That's very common," Scott responded. "But it's avoidable. One of the most effective ways to control your business development process from the very beginning is to set a strong agenda with your prospective clients, which leads me to this magazine photo."

Scott passed the magazine to Cheryl.

"Imagine that we're having a Thanksgiving dinner at our conference table here, but imagine it doesn't look anything like this photo. Here, our table is just a slab of wood, and there's no linen, china, or silverware to be found. As the host, I bring out a beautiful brown turkey for everyone to admire, dump it on the middle of the table, and then slap the cranberries, stuffing and sweet potatoes right on top!"

"You'd probably be pretty astonished, right?" Scott laughed. "That's not the way Thanksgiving is supposed to be. Or maybe it is at your families' tables; I shouldn't assume," Scott joked.

Everyone was smiling now at the crazy notion of a pile of food in the middle of a Thanksgiving table.

Scott motioned to the magazine being passed around the room. "Now focus on this Thanksgiving table. It's beautifully prepared with silverware, china and linens. The turkey and all the sides are properly presented; there are no surprises and everyone is happy. It's a stark contrast between the two meals—much like it would be in a sales meeting in which the salesperson just wings it and does whatever comes to mind at the time. But when a salesperson properly sets up the business meeting with a strong agenda, it always becomes a more productive use of everyone's time. Unfortunately, most business development professionals don't use agendas in their sales process."

Dan caught Scott's eye and gave him a sheepish look. "I have to admit that although I use agendas for business meetings, I don't set them for prospective client meetings. I don't want to appear overbearing."

Scott nodded. "You do have to be careful about *how* you set the agenda," he said. "How you say things can ultimately be as important as the actual words themselves. It's imperative to have a nurturing, but confident tone from the beginning and to get permission from the prospect before proceeding. I have six steps that will help you establish and execute a strong sales agenda."

Scott turned to the whiteboard and wrote:

"The first thing we need to do is ask our prospects for permission to set an agenda. By asking for permission, we are getting their buy-in with respect to what's coming next. The way we say this makes it very difficult for the prospect to reject our idea of an agenda. For example, I would say, 'In order to make the best use of our time today, would it be okay if I set a brief agenda for us?' They will always agree, because no one is thinking, 'Gee, I really want to waste my time right now.'"

Once you've obtained agreement on the idea of an agenda, proceed to ask for 60 minutes of uninterrupted time, ideally in a quiet place without distractions. I like to ask for 60 minutes, however others might ask for less time based on the type of sale or people they are meeting. Without a time limit set ahead of time, the prospect can easily cut your time short. But by agreeing on a certain amount of distraction-free time, you can keep your prospect's attention. Then we need to clearly determine why we are meeting this person, and why this person is meeting us. Generally, we want the prospect to agree that we are there to see if there's a *fit* for our services or a reason to do business."

Scott sat back at the table. "Steps three and four are related. It's important to share with your prospect that you're going to be asking targeted questions so that you can understand his needs and challenges. Then we want to ask him what his expectations are for the meeting. Doing so could help you uncover a problem he has, and it will help make his intentions for the meeting clear. Once expectations are established on both sides, we can determine what each of us is looking for as an outcome of the meeting."

Scott smiled at the group. "Here's a question for you all. What's the number one thing you hate to hear in a sales meeting?" he asked.

"That's easy," Stacey said. "When a prospect says 'no.' As I've mentioned before, I hear that a lot."

"That's what most business developers say. As we spoke about earlier, we take that 'no' personally and think it's the worst possible thing we can hear. Must be your high 'I' at work here right, Stacey," Scott joked. "But I disagree. The worst possible answer is 'I need to think about it.' Indecision is the *worst* enemy for business development people, because more often than not, the prospect means 'no.' He just doesn't want to tell you directly. Why do you think that is?"

Cheryl interjected. "They just don't want to hurt your feelings or they're trying to string you along for free information."

"Exactly," said Scott. "Or, they don't want to deal with a pushy salesperson trying to convince them their decision wasn't the right one. At the end of the day, the 'I need to think about it' is really a 'no' most of the time. Not realizing that will result in you making countless follow-up phone calls and having false hope that the prospect will come around. That's why we need to be very clear with our prospects that our expectation for the outcome of the meeting is to hear a resounding 'yes' or a 'no.' They need to understand that 'no' is a perfectly acceptable answer. You also want to clearly define the next step. A 'yes' could be a next meeting or the prospect introducing his business partner to you, or it could be a check and contract. Either way, you have to move the prospect forward to a next step or end the meeting as friends. Failure to agree on a next step forward with a prospect is one of the greatest mistakes made by any sales professional."

Scott paused before moving on to the last step.

"This last step, using takeaways, is actually built in throughout the agenda. Takeaways allow us to maintain control of the meeting. For example, once the prospect has agreed that a 'yes' or 'no' outcome is perfectly acceptable, we can take away the option to 'think about it.' To do this, we need the prospect to clearly understand that a 'no' is an acceptable end result and that a 'think about it' is not and why. Another takeaway could happen on the phone if we use an agenda prior to the meeting. We might ask the prospect: 'Other than a real emergency, is there any reason we would not be meeting next week?'

Here we are trying to protect our time from a prospect who might cancel at the last minute. Getting them to verbalize that nothing short of an emergency would stop our meeting from occurring is another verbal commitment for which we can hold him accountable. Protecting your time is so important; it literally is money."

Scott looked over at Dan, who nodded and smiled.

"Yeah, when you're billing hourly, everything you do is looked at in terms of what you could be billing. Time is always money to me."

"And you only have a limited amount of it each week. Cancelled meetings happen, but they will happen a lot less if all of our steps are followed."

Scott saw his clients following but wanted to get them more involved in the discussion.

"Let's do a quick role play before we end the day," he said. "Dan, why don't you come up here with me?"

Looking less than thrilled, Dan joined Scott at the front of the room.

"Ok, Dan's my prospect. Let's assume we have spent five-to-ten minutes building some rapport at the beginning of our business meeting. At this point, Dan, you like and trust me. Then I would say, 'Dan, I know we set a brief agenda on the phone last week, but would it be alright to just recap it again now that we are together?'"

"Sure Scott," Dan played along.

"Great," Scott responded. "As discussed, we'll need about sixty minutes to discuss your current situation and how I may be of assistance. We still have about fifty minutes left, are we okay for that amount of time?"

"Yes, that's great."

"Perfect. The purpose of our meeting, as I see it, is to determine if there is a fit for us to work together. In order to find that out, I'll be asking several questions about your business. Just want to make sure you're okay with that?'

"Sure" Dan said.

Scott continued, "I may also ask you some tough questions as well, and I want to make sure that's okay."

"That's fine," Dan said. "I'll do my best to answer them."

"Thanks, Dan. Anything specific you want to make sure we cover today?"

"Just to learn more about your services, Scott," Dan replied.

"Great, we'll certainly cover that later in the meeting today. So, at the end of our time together Dan, typically one of a few things will happen.

We may decide that there's a great fit and agree to proceed with a specific next step, or one or both of us may determine that there really isn't a good fit, and that the potential of our working together may end in a 'no.' Are you okay telling me 'no' if that's the case?"

"Sure. I'm good at saying 'no.'"

"Okay, that's great, Dan. Because occasionally at the end of a meeting, people might tell me that they want to think about it or that they'll get back to me. In most of those cases, they're really telling me they're not interested, but they don't want to hurt my feelings. The truth is, I'd actually prefer it if people just gave me an honest 'no.' I would really appreciate it if you could be straight with me if there isn't a fit, and I assure you I'll be straight with you if I don't see a good fit here. Is that okay?"

"That would be terrific," Dan agreed. "I am a pretty straight shooter as you'll see."

Scott stepped away from Dan. "As you can see, I'm working to control the tempo and direction of the meeting so that I don't waste my time, money and emotional energy on the wrong people and opportunities. The key here is to make the agenda feel collaborative, not aggressive or manipulative in any way. By setting a strong agenda, you'll be moving both parties toward a favorable outcome, while controlling the sales process every time. By the way, did any of you keep track of how many times he agreed with me during the agenda?"

"I counted four or five times," Cheryl said.

"Correct," Scott said. "There are a number of perks with this strategy. First, we are controlling the meeting by asking questions. Second, when they agree to things we say, like answering tough questions, we can hold them accountable when we do actually ask the difficult questions. Also, we gave the prospect permission to say 'no.' This is incredibly powerful as the prospect will relax and feel less threatened that you are there to close a sale. Lastly, we are conditioning the prospect to follow our lead. These four factors will dramatically improve the quality of your meetings. You'll highlight your professionalism and will stand out compared to other competitors with whom they may be speaking."

"Scott, I understand your point about controlling the meeting, but the script you suggest sounds a little mechanical to me," Stacey said. "I'm not sure that I could really see myself saying these things."

"That's a valid concern, Stacey," Scott responded. "Like most new things you try, this is going to feel uncomfortable at first. But remember, this is a proven methodology for controlling meetings. Setting the time, discussing expectations and agreeing on outcomes will help you set the table. It only sounds mechanical right now because you haven't practiced it and you haven't taken ownership of the language yet. I definitely suggest altering the language a little to better reflect your style. You can certainly add fillers to soften the tone or adapt it to your speaking style in other ways. Tweak it to make it your own and make it feel more natural or conversational, but make sure you're still hitting all of the steps. Once you get comfortable with running your meetings in this manner, you're going to feel a better flow to your meetings. And if things get off track, you're going to be a in a much better position to bring it back on course."

"I have another question," Dan said when Scott finished his explanation for Stacey. "Can I just email the agenda ahead of time?"

"You know, Dan, I'd really advise against that," Scott said. "Remember, we're getting verbal approval and commitments as we're setting the agenda. Those verbal commitments are important for conditioning the prospect to say 'yes' and agree with our suggested program. An email would be a last resort because the agenda won't be nearly as effective as one set in person or over the phone."

"Okay, it's getting late, so let's do a quick wrap-up today. For your homework, practice going through a conversation where you set the agenda. See how you can make it your own while also working in those key points like setting expectations and getting permission to ask tough questions. Now in just a few words, can you all share what struck you as most important today?"

"A formal agenda is the control element for your meeting and it covers all the bases for a productive meeting," Cheryl said.

"Get your prospect's approval as you go through each piece of the agenda," Stacey added. "It forces them to commit to next steps with you."

Dan added the last point. "Highlight to the prospect that it's okay to say 'no.' This point is personal for me as my time is literally money. Any chance I get to move someone to a 'no' early on in the process is perfect for me. Chasing someone around who isn't going to move forward is a huge time waster for me."

"Perfect," Scott said. "Once you start practicing and implementing this technique, you'll have more control over your meetings and you'll be in a stronger position to close new business."

WEEK 5:
QUESTIONING TO DRIVE URGENCY

———

Scott's clients were seated and chatting with one another when he entered the conference room the following week.

"Good morning," Cheryl said as she looked up from her conversation with Stacey and Dan. "We were just talking about you."

"All good things, I hope," Scott said with a smile.

"We were just curious about how you got started in the sales coaching business," Cheryl responded.

"Yeah, we were wondering why you decided to give away your secrets," Dan joked.

Scott put down his papers and joined his clients at the table. "Well I don't really consider it giving away my secrets. I got into sales coaching as a way to help other business professionals. I know it sounds hokey, but I really wanted to do something in my career that would help other people succeed although I have to admit that wasn't my main goal when I started in sales. But I had one of those life-altering experiences that make you look at things in a different light."

His clients' eyes widened.

"What happened to you?" Cheryl asked, intrigued.

"I was in a plane crash."

"Excuse me," said Dan. "Did you just say 'plane crash'?"

"That's right." Scott was used to people being surprised when he mentioned the crash.

"Though the story is best told over a cold beer, I think it would be a good one for me to share with you now. A number of years ago, I was a passenger on a private rented plane heading back from a weekend away when—without warning—we suddenly lost our engine. As you can imagine, hearing a sputtering noise on a one-engine airplane is never good."

Cheryl looked over nervously at Scott. "You must have been terrified," she said.

"We all were. I can still remember the terror on the faces of my fellow passengers. Everyone looked to one another as the severity of our situation set in. In the cockpit, the pilot was desperately trying to get the engine started again, while also looking for anywhere he could to put us down safely. I tried my best to stay calm, but everyone was panicked as the ground started rushing toward us. I remember looking out the window, seeing trees and then—nothing."

Scott paused before finishing the story. Even though he'd told the story hundreds of times, it was a difficult memory.

"When I woke up, there was commotion all around me. Flashing lights and sirens filled my senses at first; then the pain set in. The plane had crash landed into a house in a suburban neighborhood. We were upside down, and the plane was ripped apart. As for me, I was lying on my right side with my left leg and arm dislocated from my body. My three broken ribs made it hard to breathe, and my right arm was all but shattered underneath me. I had never really known pain until the firefighters pulled me out of there. To this day, I have never felt pain as severe as I felt at that moment."

Dan winced. "That sounds awful. You'd never know by looking at you now that you'd been so badly injured."

"My physical and psychological recoveries took a long time," Scott responded. "I was in a wheelchair without the use of my arms for over two months. I felt helpless, and I doubted whether I would be able to do all the things I had done before the crash. But I was determined to regain my strength. The full recovery took more than four months. During that recovery, I had plenty of time to think. Although I had never been all that spiritual, I realized that I had been given a gift by surviving the crash. And I really wanted to do something in my life to make that gift worthwhile. Every morning when I wake up, I feel so thankful for the opportunity I have been given. Too many people wake up every day and take life for granted. They squander their time by spending it complaining, dwelling on the negative or living in a state of apathy. I have to admit I was living that way myself before the accident. It's really unfortunate that it takes something so dramatic to get someone like me to change."

Cheryl caught Scott's eye.

"That's definitely not the story we expected to hear about how you got into the coaching business," she said.

"The crash really did change my life and set me on the path to where I am today," said Scott. "I started my business because I wanted to offer a solution—a second chance—to struggling business professionals. Many of my clients come to me when they're lost or ready to throw in the towel on whatever venture they've started.

Others reach out because they are looking to take things to the next level. Through my coaching, I give them the tools and support they need to succeed and reach their fullest potentials. And I feel really good about helping them achieve their sales goals so their businesses can thrive."

Scott was eager to start the morning. "Alright, enough about me," he said. "Let's get the day going. Did anyone get a chance to set a formal agenda in your meetings last week?"

"I didn't have any meetings last week," Dan said. "I really need to get my activity up."

"I did try it, Scott," Stacey said. "I set a few agendas on the phone before my meetings, and I felt like I was portraying a more professional image."

"I did, too," Cheryl said. "Although it sounded a little robotic at first, I have to admit that it worked. My prospect agreed to everything, and the agenda helped me keep the meeting on track. But I think I'm going to have to keep practicing so that the dialogue within the agenda sounds more conversational."

"Exactly," Scott replied. "You want the prospect to feel like you're having a conversation and that you're setting the agenda together. The more you practice, the better it will flow. Okay, let's move on to some new material."

As his clients flipped open their notes from the previous week, Scott drew a picture on the board to illustrate his next point.

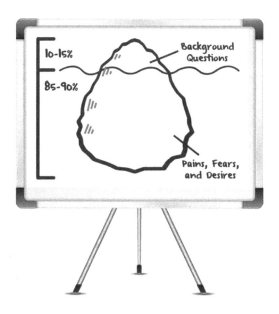

Cheryl, Dan and Stacey looked up at his drawing and then to Scott as he walked back toward them.

"Last week we talked about the foundation for successful business development, including preparation and the basic elements we need to establish for any prospect meeting," he said. "Today we're going to talk about what I consider to be the most important aspect of the sales process. What you're going to learn is so important because the landscape of sales has changed. Long gone are the days of the killer presentation or the easy request for proposal. In today's challenging selling environment, only one selling strategy can consistently win the day. Ironically enough, it requires no selling at all."

Scott smiled as his clients looked at each other skeptically.

"In order to obtain business from a new client, business development professionals must effectively identify or uncover their prospect's real issues," Scott said emphatically. "But most business developers don't have that skill—because they've never been trained how to ask effective questions."

Scott slid over to the whiteboard and in large letters, wrote:

QUESTIONING

"The majority of business developers don't ask nearly enough questions of their prospects," he explained. "Instead, they charge right in—eagerly selling and presenting with the hope that the prospect hears something he likes. Sure, if someone is a legal expert, for example, it's easiest to sell by talking about what you know best—the law. But that approach doesn't always work anymore. It's unfocused and, more often than not, only results in us providing some unpaid consulting as prospects try to pull out information, pricing and a proposal. Asking tough questions is the only way to uncover your prospect's fears, needs and desires—the critical motivators for them to want to pursue next steps with you."

Scott shifted backward and motioned to his rendering of an iceberg on the board. "You're probably wondering about the tie-in to the iceberg I just drew on the board. We all know the phrase, 'tip of the iceberg,' which alludes to how difficult it can be to judge the size and shape of an iceberg by the tip that's visible above the water. Our prospects are like icebergs—so much important information lies beneath the surface of what our prospects initially want to share with us. We have to find out what lurks beneath and make a concerted effort to discover the underlying factors that will drive our prospects to pursue a relationship with us."

Approaching the group again, Scott continued. "Unfortunately, most salespeople, even experienced ones, have a hard time getting below the surface when they're talking with prospects. First, this is due to them dominating most of the conversation by presenting to prospects all about their company, features and benefits, etc. Keep in mind, most salespeople have no idea what the prospects needs, pains or desires are."

Second, as I just alluded to, most salespeople have a hard time getting below the surface since they're usually not asking enough—or the right—questions. They only ask surface questions, such as easy background questions about the organization's history, location, competition or current vendors. Those questions are fine, and they do provide us with some understanding of the prospect's business issues, but they generally only result in superficial answers. And these days we need to know a lot more than that to win a new client. Without skillful questioning and listening, getting new clients to move off the dime is usually a tough challenge."

Stacey leaned forward. "It sounds like you want us to play the role of psychiatrist," she said.

"In a way," Scott responded. "The mantra for our process needs to be 'prescription before diagnosis is malpractice.' In other words, we must effectively diagnose our prospects thoroughly before providing the proper prescription. Failure to do this can lead to the wrong prescription, or in your case, the wrong proposal. We must start this process at the tip of the iceberg by asking the background questions, like the ones I just mentioned a minute ago. What do you all think are some good background questions for your prospective buyers?"

Stacey responded first. "How about, 'Who is currently providing your plumbing supplies?'"

"Here's one," Cheryl said. "Tell me about your current IT infrastructure?"

"Dan, how about you?" Scott asked.

"Sure, I would ask about the prospect's business and the growth he's seen in the last few years, or I'd ask how the person got started in the business."

"All good background questions," Scott remarked. "It's really important to remember that we have to start the questioning step with light and easy questions to get the prospect warmed up. Starting the questioning process with difficult or probing questions is a mistake; it's too much, too soon. Once you've completed your background questions, it's time to take a little deeper dive into the prospect's issues, needs or wants. Mainly, you have to come prepared with a strong questioning process that will reveal a prospect's deeper motivations—like the pain he's facing or the reasons why he absolutely needs to find a solution to a particular problem. In order to have a solid case for a prospective client to work with you, we need to uncover at least two or more issues to be solved. Getting to those issues is kind of like getting a conviction in a murder trial. I know this might seem like an extreme analogy, but it actually is a good way to demonstrate what I'm talking about. In order to convict a suspect of a major crime, what do you need to get a conviction?"

Dan was first to respond. "Evidence might help."

"How about a murder weapon or a witness," Stacey added.

"All key ingredients to an effective prosecution," Scott continued. "You need proof that the suspect committed the murder. If you only have minimal evidence, the suspect is going to go free. But if you have several proof points—like a strong witness, DNA and a confession, you're going to win that case. That idea can be applied to what we need to ascertain about our prospective clients. If we don't uncover their issues, or if we heard only one problem they're facing, they might not have a strong enough reason to do business with us. On the other hand, if we have three or four reasons for them to change something that isn't working for them, then we know we have a good case for them to hire us to solve it. Typically, you need to obtain a minimum of three or four reasons or pain points to make your meeting with a prospect truly worthwhile. So after the prospect responds with a problem, always ask 'What else?' and then continue getting a list of his problems, frustrations and challenges. The more problems and frustrations you uncover, the more opportunity or motivation there will be solve the problems."

Cheryl raised her hand. "What if you have a client who starts dumping all of his problems on you, even if they aren't relevant to what you provide?"

"That's a good question, Cheryl, and it leads me to my next point. As you're gathering your prospect's business issues, it's important to prioritize those issues. Doing so can help you reign in someone who's getting off topic," Scott advised. "Ask him what problems are most damaging or troubling, and work down the list. That way you spend the majority of your time focused on the issues that are most important to him. Our goal is to identify and prioritize three to five issues."

"What happens if you're only able to uncover one issue during your questioning?" Dan asked.

"Here's an idea that will help you avoid a meeting where you only uncover one issue. And, since I'm on a roll with analogies today, here's one more. Cheryl, do me a favor. As fast as you can, list five items on the McDonald's menu?"

Cheryl quickly responded: "Big Mac, Filet-O-Fish, fries, cheeseburger and a chocolate shake."

"Eat there often?" Dan teased.

"No!" Cheryl smiled. "But I have eaten my fair share."

"Okay, so let me tell you all why this is relevant to finding issues," Scott said. "We all know the McDonald's menu by heart practically, yet we may not have thought about the top issues our prospective clients typically face. This is important because when you are struggling to identify a prospect's issues, you can refer back to a mental list or menu of issues that you know other clients and prospects often cite. For example, I know that most of my prospective clients lack a real plan to achieve their goals, invest too much time in the wrong places with the wrong people or struggle to get in the door because of tough gatekeepers."

"Hallelujah," Stacey added. "That's one of mine."

"Exactly," Scott responded. "I have a mental list of all of your probable issues before you even share them with me. Keeping that list in the front of my mind is important because when I meet with someone who is not being very forthcoming with me, I can tell him about other clients I've helped and the issues they were facing. It's a strong technique because it prevents you from being accusatory. You're not saying that the prospect in front of you has these problems; you're just sharing them as examples. And you'll likely open his mind to other issues he might not have thought of until you mentioned them."

"Can you walk us through how that would sound, Scott?" Cheryl asked.

"Sure thing, Cheryl. Let's say you're my prospect. I might say 'Cheryl, I understand that one of your main issues is gatekeepers holding you back. What else is an issue for you regarding your business development efforts?' Now let's say that Cheryl says, 'I'm not sure Scott.' I would be stuck at one issue right? We need to be more persistent. So I'd say, 'Cheryl, I'm not sure that these are issues for you, but many of my clients in the past have told me that they struggle with getting in front of the real decision makers, wasting too much time on proposals that never get signed or dealing with prospects that want to negotiate price. I'm just curious, are any of those issues for you as well?' See what I did there? When Cheryl agrees, we just went from having one issue to three or four. Being prepared with your own business version of a McDonald's menu can ultimately lead to better and more effective sales meetings."

Scott looked over at Dan. "As a lawyer, Dan, you have to ask good questions to uncover the information you need to win cases, right?"

"Absolutely," he responded.

"So if you're trying to identify a prospect's pains, fears or desires, what questions come to mind that we should ask?"

Dan paused for a moment to think about it.

"I suppose I would ask more specific questions, like how long a problem has been going on, what they've done to fix it in the past, and why they think the problem exists in the first place."

Scott nodded. "Those are great questions, Dan. We also could ask how much the problem costs the company and what other impact it's having on the company and on the prospect personally. Always be prepared with open-ended questions that will keep the prospect talking. Again, our goal should not only be to discover their issues, but also to hear how those issues have affected the prospect's life."

Scott went back to the whiteboard and quickly wrote:

FIND PAIN.

"Most importantly, we need to ask questions that are designed to help us find our prospect's pain. Once we have our issues list, or the prospect's frustrations, concerns or challenges, we should be prepared to take the deeper dive and go below the water's surface. Now it's time to investigate the bottom of the iceberg, which is where the majority of the opportunity can be found."

"Scott, once I uncover some of the prospect's pain, why can't I just sell him on the spot?" Dan asked.

"Good question, Dan, and I understand the instinct to immediately go into sales mode. But we have to make sure we find enough pain in order to build our case to the point that it warrants a high level of commitment to move forward on our solution. That's why premature presentation isn't a good idea, and that's why it's so important to keep digging and put a real case together instead of immediately trying to solve something that looks promising. Again, we want to have three to five apparent reasons ready to go at a moment's notice."

Scott paused as his clients jotted down more notes.

"I want to take a step back for a minute, because finding the prospect's true pain isn't easy," Scott said. "In fact, it's one of the toughest parts of business development. After all, it's a lot easier to go into a meeting and toss out the features and benefits of your services. Unfortunately, that's not effective anymore. The real challenge is to go in, ask great questions and find the reasons for the prospect to work with you to solve his issues. Although finding needs is important, more often than not, needs aren't enough to motivate your prospect to move quickly forward with you. Earlier, I mentioned asking about how a problem affects a prospect personally. That's a really important tactic, but it takes a little bit of courage to ask the probing questions you need to really understand how your prospects' business issues might be affecting him personally."

Stacey smiled wryly. "Sometimes it's easy if you get a person rolling. Most people love to talk about themselves," she noted.

"Absolutely true," Scott said. "And people typically make decisions for one reason: themselves! The thought that the solution will help his company will always be secondary to an *individual's* needs, fears and pains. So when you're in a meeting, look for discomfort in the prospect's body language or a change in his tone. Key in on those clues. Write down any emotional words he uses. Get your prospect to verbalize his pain so that you can understand how serious he is about solving the challenges."

Scott wrote two more words on the board:

FEAR
GAIN

"Pain is the greatest motivator, but there are two other factors that shouldn't be left out: fear and gain. Because sometimes, a prospect just doesn't have any pains at the time that you're meeting with him. Business may be running smoothly at the time. In that case, it's important to identify what fears he has about keeping things running well or to find out what he wants to accomplish and gain in the future."

Cheryl caught Scott's attention. "Scott, I usually shy away from getting too personal in my business dealings, but it sounds like I may be missing out on picking up some emotional cues."

"Very likely," Scott said, appreciating Cheryl's feedback. "From a young age, we've all been taught not to ask personal questions. But in sales, far and away the fastest way to get business is to find out something personal about your prospect and show how your solution could help solve a problem. In so many cases, a sale comes down to the personal connection level. There are business issues and there are personal issues, but it's usually the personal issues that lead to a decision to make change happen. Like I said, people make decisions for personal and emotional reasons. Then they back up those decisions with logic. And the larger the decision, the more emotion is needed for a prospect to lean one direction or another. It's your responsibility to look below the surface and uncover those reasons that will compel your prospect to take action. So, Cheryl, try to overcome your fears about asking personal questions. As long as it's done in a soft and nurturing way, it isn't rude, and it actually can improve your relationship with your prospects."

"So what do we do if we are not able to uncover any compelling reasons or pain Scott," Stacey asked. "Great question Stacey," Scott said. "This might be a good time to look at your options. First, are you a hundred percent sure you asked enough of the right questions? Do you need to keep digging? Or, is this a time to do a take-away."

"What the heck is that?" Dan inquired.

"A take-away is when you remove yourself from the situation. Think about what happens when you take a toy away from a child. They cry to get it back, right? Now, I don't expect any prospects of yours breaking down in tears, however in some circumstances they will fight to get you back. Mainly because they like and trust you, but for the most part it's because you still haven't given them your solutions. Remember, that's the power, if any, that you hold over your prospects. If you were to use a take-away, it might sound something like this; 'Listen Bob, I appreciate your answering some of my questions. However, based on the limited information you've shared with me, it's very difficult to understand if we are indeed a fit to work together. If you recall, we had agreed earlier in our meeting that if one or both of us didn't feel that there was a fit that we would be straight with each other and let the other one know. I think we might be at that point now. I do want to thank you for your time today though.' So as you can see, it's okay to sometimes call a prospect out on not being forthcoming with us and letting him know that you might walk away. In many cases, they will open up at that point and give you the pain, fear or gain that you need in order to know that there are reasons to work together. Does that make sense to everyone?"

The group nodded in agreement. Scott continued, "The key is to move the prospect forward or go back to better understand why he isn't moving forward and address it. Hiding from the truth or the lies doesn't help you win in sales. Alright, let's wrap up for the day. Remember, in the agenda step, you brought up the fact that you'd be asking tough questions, and you got the prospect's 'ok', so you already have permission to go to some deeper places. Over the course of the next week, I'd really like everyone to practice asking some tougher questions in your meetings. Okay, let's do some quick AHAs. Stacey, why don't you start?"

"Well, apart from learning that you were in a plane crash, I learned that I need to be asking a lot more questions than I ever have before. And those questions need to be focused on uncovering my prospects' problems. I can't just go into a meeting thinking I'm going to present my solutions right away."

"Good. What about you, Dan?" Scott asked.

"I'm going to be working on uncovering a longer list of my prospect's issues. I think that will help me avoid getting stuck in a meeting without enough ammunition for why the prospect needs my services. And it sends the urgency factor way up."

"It definitely will help. And you, Cheryl?"

"I'm going to dig much deeper and try to find out how my prospects are being personally affected by their business issues. I think this is going to be the key to the entire selling process for me now."

"Those are great AHAs, everybody," Scott said. "I guarantee that you'll get more comfortable with questioning your prospects more deeply once you've had a chance to work on this skill. And once people start sharing more intimate information with you, you'll see how much more targeted you can be in your proposals and how much faster you'll get business."

WEEK 6:
OBTAINING COMMITMENT

———

Scott's clients were ready to get down to business the following week. He took that as a good sign. They were getting more invested and confident in the program as each week passed.

"Tell me about your first attempts at questioning prospects to find their pain," he encouraged.

Dan leaned forward. "Scott, I had some good success with questioning last week. Normally I'd go into my pitch right away, but this time, I tried your method. I asked much better, more in-depth questions, and I uncovered a lot more information about my prospect's needs and desires."

"I'm glad to hear that, Dan."

"I did a lot more listening last week, too," Cheryl said. "I'd say I spent 80 percent of my time listening to my prospects' responses to my questions and only 20 percent of my time talking. That was a big turnaround for me."

"I had an interesting experience last week," Stacey added. "When I started questioning a prospect more diligently, I realized he didn't have a real need for my product. He was only meeting with me to kick tires and find out my pricing on a few specific plumbing supplies. He wasn't a serious buyer, and I saved a lot of time by recognizing that and moving him more quickly to a 'no.'"

Scott smiled. "It sounds like everyone had some positive experiences last week and that's terrific. Now, once we know what's going to motivate our prospects to make a change, we need to get them to commit to following through. I'd like to spend our time today talking about commitment, since it's the lifeblood of developing new business. From the time we begin to establish a new relationship with our prospects to when we take them on as new clients, we should always be asking for commitment. The answers our prospects give to our commitment questions help us gauge whether the prospect is qualified to work with us."

Joining his clients at the table again, Scott said, "Let's discuss why people commit to things.

I'll start with two extreme examples. Imagine you're riding your bike on a beautiful summer day, when all of a sudden, a car cuts you off and you lose your balance. You flip off your bike and land on your arm, snapping it. Badly hurt and in a lot of pain, do you go home and forget it happened, or do you immediately commit to a hospital visit? Or, let's say you're a pack-a-day smoker and you're at the doctor for your annual physical. After the exam, the doctor delivers bad news, telling you that you'll only live another six months if you don't quit smoking. That type of news is going to spark a pretty big commitment on your part to quit smoking. Obviously situations with our prospects aren't nearly so dire, but we still need to ascertain their commitment to make a change."

Scott shifted his chair to the right to face Stacey. "Here's a business example for you. Let's say I'm sitting with a prospective client like Stacey here, and we're discussing her sales issues. I ask some tough questions and find out that her closing rate and activity levels are extremely low. I even find out that if she doesn't grow her book of business, she's likely going to be passed over for a promotion. Not only that, she tells me that her spouse has been laid off and they're facing a very tight cash situation at home."

Scott turned back to the group as he continued. "I kept digging deeper until I got the prospect to verbalize her pain. If she says it, she owns it, and that's the best way to obtain commitment from a prospect. If she can't verbalize her pain and commit to fixing her issues, she's not going to be as viable a prospect, and we're wasting our time and energy on the wrong person. Our solutions aren't going to be a priority, and she'll likely just put off a decision. This leaves us hoping she will eventually come around, while we waste a lot of time on useless follow-up calls that never get returned."

Scott paused to let his points sink in. He could tell there were still some questions rolling around in his clients' heads, so he decided to add in an analogy that would help. "Let's take a step back and consider what we've done prior to asking a strong commitment question. We started with some background questions, moved through some business issues and finally found a number of compelling reasons for our prospect to change his current situation. Think about the urgency level of your prospect when you first met."

Scott drew a sketch of a meter on the board.

"Imagine that when your prospective client meets with you, they are near the bottom of our urgency meter. The bottom of the meter is defined as having 'no interest' in changing his current situation and the top is defined as a 'must change' situation. By asking questions that draw out his pains, fears and desires, you can actually work your prospect up the urgency meter to the top. Think about it, without a compelling reason to change, most people will just stay in their current situation, or in this case, they'll stay with their current vendor. Let me ask you all something. What are some things that would make it urgent for me to run out of this room right now?"

"If you were tired of dealing with us," Dan teased

"Well that's certainly one possibility, Dan," Scott shot back with a smile.

"There might be a fire," Stacey added.

"Right on the money, Stacey," Scott complimented. "Or maybe I look out the window and see someone who needs help. These are urgent scenarios that drive action. We need this type of emotional response to help drive actions from our prospective clients. Finding their issues, costs and emotional reasons to change drives their urgency level up and allows change to happen. Does that help?"

"It really does. So, Scott, what would you consider good commitment-type questions?" Stacey asked.

"There are a lot of ways to ask for commitment, Stacey, and I recommend being very direct in your questioning. Ask your prospect if his issues are 'could', 'should' or 'must-fix' issues. Or have him rate his commitment to change by asking: On a scale of 1 to 10, how committed are you to fixing these problems? Or, try: What priority level would you put on fixing these problems? And finally, you could ask him straight out: Do you want my help in solving these issues?"

Stacey nodded as she wrote down Scott's examples.

"Using a few of these commitment questions will help you better understand what your prospect is thinking or feeling about solving the problems. Without a verbal expression from your prospect, it's always going to be a guessing game about when a deal will close or if the prospect will ever return a voice mail you left. Your ability to find pain and get a commitment from your prospect is the cornerstone of successfully gaining new business. And here's a good tip: Verbally recap all of the pain, fears and possible gains you uncovered in your conversations before asking your commitment questions. By repeating those factors back to your prospect in his own words, you show that you were listening and that you completely understand his issues, and he'll be more likely to commit to a solution."

"Scott, isn't it a bit early to ask for a commitment?" Cheryl asked. "At this point, I haven't even presented my services."

"Cheryl, keep in mind that we're not asking for the order at this time," Scott responded. "Rather, we're defining whether this is a problem that he wants to fix and whether he wants our help to do so. So, is he committed to solving his problem? And does he want our help to fix it? In the prospect's mind, we are already the best choice because of his *belief* in us. Even though we haven't shared solutions yet, we have built a tremendous amount of trust because we have asked all the right questions. The prospect will assuredly believe that we have a targeted solution. Do you see the distinction here?"

"I do, thanks."

Dan leaned forward to catch Scott's attention. "What happens if we don't get a commitment from our prospect? What if we ask questions and uncover his issues and pain but have a hard time getting him to commit to fixing the problems?"

"That happens occasionally, Dan, and it's important for us to address it. If your prospect is resistant to fixing the problem, ask yourself if you really uncovered the pain. If not, go back and find it. If you did identify the pain, then it's very possible your prospect isn't being totally honest with you about his situation or his desire for your solutions. But that's where asking these commitment questions becomes so useful," Scott explained enthusiastically. "It gives you the opportunity to air out objections, stalls, and lies. Obviously, our goal here is to solve must-fix problems. Recognize that either you might need to put in more work to uncover pain, or you probably aren't dealing with someone who's being a hundred percent straight with you. So you might not be headed toward a positive outcome."

Scott looked around at his clients. "Isn't it better to know that your prospective client isn't being truthful with you early on in the process versus two or three meetings in?" he asked. "If you know what's real or not real with your prospective client early on, you're in a much better position to handle it or get the prospect to a quick 'no' decision before you waste any more time, energy or money."

"Absolutely," Dan agreed. "The last thing I want to do is waste time."

"Getting commitment at this point in the process is critical to keep us moving in a forward direction; practice being soft- but direct- in your commitment questions. This week, go out and try to drive someone to make a commitment whether that means a next meeting or moving forward to work together," he said, noticing they were running short on time. "Okay, AHA moments for today."

"I liked your examples about why people commit to things," Stacey said. "I'm going to keep those in the back of my mind as I'm talking to prospects. You can't move forward without understanding your prospect's commitment to change his existing situation. Otherwise you're just providing free consulting."

"I'm going to be more direct in my approach in evaluating prospects' commitment," Cheryl added. I'm going to start asking straight out whether they are absolutely committed to fixing their problems once I better understand them. I think that will help me weed out wishy-washy prospects."

"I agree," Dan said. "I'm going to concentrate on pulling out those urgent, must-fix scenarios with all my prospects. If you don't find that urgency, they probably won't commit the time, money and energy to my solution anyway."

"Excellent," Scott said. "We're going to be talking more about testing our prospects' ability to move forward in a couple of weeks. For now, I want you to focus on finding out if they are committed to solving the problem and whether they think you are the person who can help them solve it. Getting commitment on those two points is critical to determining whether you can continue with the meeting or if there's more you need to address."

WEEK 7:
GETTING TO THE DECISION MAKER

———

"**A**lright, last week we left off talking about commitment, asking the questions that will help us identify the motivators for our prospects to take action," Scott said as he opened the next session. "Did anyone get a solid commitment out of a prospect?"

Stacey looked up. "I had some confusion on this step. I asked one of my prospects about her commitment to fixing her plumbing problem and she said it was a 'could fix.' I didn't know what to do."

"Did you draw out any compelling reasons for why the problem needed to be fixed? Did you find the emotional or personal reasons for why she needed to change what she was currently doing?" Scott asked.

"No, I guess not really."

"Okay, remember, you never want to ask whether it's a 'should', 'could' or 'must-fix' problem if you don't have the compelling reasons to make it a 'must-fix.' Don't move to the commitment step until you thoroughly understand whether the problems are pressing and how you can provide a solution. A better way to handle it might be doing a '1 to 10 assessment'," Scott advised. "For example, ask your prospect: 'On a scale of 1 to 10, with 10 being highly committed to fixing this problem, where would you say are?' If she says she's a 2 or 3, then obviously she's not committed at all, and you might not have done a good job in the questioning step. If she says she's a 7 or 8, you know you're on the right track and you can reinforce that it's a 'must-fix'. So there are ways to ask the commitment questions differently if you don't think you're quite there yet. Does that make sense, Stacey?"

"It does. Now I see that I should have dug deeper."

"Don't worry. It takes time to really understand and apply these techniques, but you'll get the hang of it. What I'd like to talk about today is making sure we're questioning the correct person. And for business developers, there's only one correct person with whom we should be talking—the decision maker."

Stacey raised her eyebrows. "I've struggled with finding the decision makers. I know it's important, but being in the plumbing business, I'm always under pressure to have a certain number of prospect meetings scheduled, so I end up meeting with whomever I can get."

Scott nodded. "Getting to the decision maker is rarely as easy as we'd like it to be. But I have several actionable tactics that you'll be able to use to get to the right person; because more often than not, if you're not talking to the decision maker or working towards him, you're wasting your time. And your ability to get to the decision maker quickly will have a huge impact on your success in generating more sales faster. So Stacey, let's use your experiences as examples here. Who do you usually find yourself talking to in a new prospect meeting?"

Stacey thought for a moment. "Well, I'm usually talking to the decision maker's gatekeeper. Or I might think I have the decision maker, but later learn that it really wasn't."

"Okay, that's really common," Scott said. "And that's why it's important that we always start by asking a few very straightforward questions. Because even if you think you have the right person, you actually might not. A lot of times, there are several layers of decision makers, or people who might influence the decision, such as board members or partners. In fact, sometimes the person you're talking to thinks he is the decision maker, but someone else is actually writing the check or signing off on the deal."

He turned to the board and wrote:

FINDING THE TRUE DECISION MAKER

· Other than yourself...
· Describe for me...
· When were you hoping...

Scott then continued, "Even if you think you're speaking to the decision maker, get in the habit of asking these three questions: First, 'Other than yourself, who else would be involved in making this decision?' Second, 'Describe for me the process you're going to go through to make this decision?' And lastly, 'What is your time frame to get the results into place?'"

"Scott, why do we have to ask about the process?" Cheryl asked. "Can't we just ask the prospect if he or she is the actual decision maker?"

"Both of these questions are important," Scott responded. "Like I mentioned, in a lot of cases, the person you're talking to might think he's the decision maker, but once you get him to start talking about the process, you might find out he needs to take it to his business partner or the board before he can make a decision. And anytime you have multiple people involved in the decision, but you're not able to talk or question them, you're putting yourself at a major disadvantage, so you really need to find that out. Ok, let's go back to Stacey. Let's say Stacey's prospect tells her that other people are involved in the decision. Don't just say 'okay' and go on. Pause the meeting and continue asking questions. This could be a deal breaker for you."

"Really?" Stacey asked skeptically.

"Yes. Pause the meeting and find out who else might be involved and what the process is going to be. Continuing on with the existing prospect isn't the best option. He's going to expect you to talk price and solutions so that he can take the details to the next person up. And the ROI, urgency and pain quickly will be lost in the translation. So I suggest politely pausing the meeting and asking if the prospect can get you in front of the real decision maker."

"How would you politely ask that?" Cheryl asked.

"Well, you could say something like 'Listen, Bob, I appreciate your interest in hearing my proposal and wanting to collect pricing for your boss, and it's no problem. But that being said, let me explain the problem I foresee with that. It's possible that when your boss sees the big price tag without really understanding the value, he might just say no. Is that a possibility?' Or, here's another suggestion," Scott continued. "You could say, 'Ok, Bob, not a problem to give you some pricing and information about my services. I have a suggestion, though. Before we take all of the time, money and energy to put a proposal together, wouldn't it make sense to have a sit-down with your boss to see what is most important to him on this project?'"

Scott looked over at Cheryl. "Make sense?" he asked.

"Yes, I suppose there are ways to push back a little bit to see if you can get in front of the decision maker."

"That's right," Scott said. "And changing the direction of the meeting to involve the real decision maker could be the big difference between success and failure in closing a new opportunity. Of course, in some situations, there might not be any other way to go. In that case, do your best to try to prepare your contact with how to deal with objections the boss might have on the proposal or fee structure. Ask how the decision maker has made decisions in the past or what are the chances that your presentation might be vetoed? The better you prepare the underling, the greater the chances you have of a positive outcome. But the unfortunate truth is that you'll be rolling the dice every time you don't directly speak to the decision maker. So try to make it a win-win every time. Either you get the order more quickly because you are speaking to the right person, or you may conclude the opportunity before wasting more time on it. Just understand that skipping this step and presenting to non-decision makers will rarely be time wisely invested. Remember that your time is money and if it isn't spent with the right decision maker, it will cost you over time."

"Okay, so this week, I want everyone to directly ask their prospects whether they are the ultimate decision makers. And follow up by asking about the decision-making process. Now let's hear some of your other AHAs from today."

"I never would have stopped a meeting before if I found out I wasn't talking to the decision maker," Stacey said. "But now that I see the meeting will likely be a waste if I don't, I'm going to start hitting pause until I get more information."

"That goes for me as well," Dan said. "I'm going to be finding out about everyone who might influence the decision and see if I can schedule time with all of them. By asking who else is involved, it prevents you from offending the person you're speaking with, while hopefully giving you the additional decision makers you need to get in front of."

"And I'm going to press for information about how they're going to be making a decision, in addition to the 'when' and 'who'," Cheryl said. "I bet I'll get a lot of great insight from those questions."

"You absolutely will, Cheryl," Scott responded. "Finding out how a decision will be made and getting in front of the right decision maker will have a huge impact on your sales results."

WEEK 8:
FINANCIALLY QUALIFYING
PROSPECTS

Arriving in the conference room a few minutes early the following week, Scott spent a few minutes thinking about his clients. They seemed to be engaged and understood his messages, but it was hard to tell for sure. Cheryl seemed to be on track, and Stacey was coming around. Dan seemed more skeptical. Scott was glad to have the mock sales meeting coming up so he could demonstrate how all the pieces of the process fit together. But for now he wanted to make sure they had a productive day. He looked up when he heard Stacey and Cheryl chatting on their way into the room. Dan was just another minute behind.

He gave everyone a few minutes to get settled before asking about their homework from the previous week.

"So how did it go when you asked your prospects if they were the final decision makers?"

"I had an interesting experience," Cheryl replied. "I asked my prospect if he was the ultimate decision maker or if anyone else was going to be involved, and he said that he'd really be the one to make the decision. But when I asked him to tell me about the process he'd be going through to make a decision, he told me that he'd be talking to a board of directors. So I realized I needed to figure out how to get in front of that board."

"This happens a lot," Scott said. Sometimes your prospects won't even realize they aren't necessarily the ultimate decision makers. Cheryl, I'd advise you to ask your prospect a few more questions about that board's involvement. For example, find out if they are just a rubber stamp of approval for your contact's decision. You could ask him if he ever brings an idea or proposal to the board that gets vetoed. If the prospect says it happens all the time, then you definitely want to make sure you find a way to get in front of that board. If he says that his recommendations always go through, then it may be okay to just coach the prospect with the key points he should make when explaining your solution to his board."

"I'm ashamed to say that I skipped the decision-making-process step in my meeting last week," Dan chimed in. "And at the end of the meeting, the person I was talking to said she was going to talk to her partner about it and give me a call."

"Did you talk through pricing with her?" Scott asked.

"Yes, I gave her some rates and additional information."

"This sounds like a case of rolling the dice and hoping for the best," Scott said. "You're basically hoping that your prospect gives the right information to her partner. However, your inability to get in front of his partner is an issue because you don't know if he has compelling reasons to fix the problem or not. Therefore, you might get a call back or you might not. Confirming you have the ultimate decision maker eliminates some of that uncertainty and risk."

"Okay, today we're going to be moving on to one of the last aspects of our process—financially qualifying our prospects," he said. "Let's imagine we're at a dinner party. What are some of the off-limit topics? Politics, religion, and usually money, right? We don't ask our fellow guests how much money they make or how much they're going to spend on their kitchen remodeling project. We've all been trained since childhood to know that it's impolite and inappropriate to talk about money in that kind of setting."

His clients nodded in agreement.

"Too many people bring that 'don't-talk-about-money mentality' into their businesses. To be successful in the business development process, we have to talk about money. We have to financially qualify our prospects and identify whether they are willing and able to make an investment with us. And there are some really important strategies we need to keep in mind, as well as questions we should be asking, when we're discussing budget and costs."

Scott walked to the center of the room to reference an earlier point. "A few weeks ago we talked about pain and uncovering the prospect's costs and losses associated with that pain," he said as he took a few steps over to his whiteboard. "When we start the money conversation, we want to go back to those losses and frustrations. For example, I might say to my client: 'You mentioned that in the past five years, these problems have cost the company more than $350,000, and that without addressing those problems, the company could easily lose another $500,000 in the next year or two, bringing us to total losses of $850,000.' Then I'd ask her how much she'd be willing and able to invest to fix an almost $1 million problem. If she didn't answer right away or tried to dodge the question, I might ask if she'd be willing to spend $500,000 or $250,000 to fix that million-dollar problem. As she's coming around to those numbers, I know in my mind that my solution is only $100,000."

Scott turned back to the board and wrote:

"The example I just gave is what I call using the direct approach. Another option is the ROI approach, where I'd ask how much a solution would be worth to the client if I could show her that the company would make $1 million by using it."

Scott motioned toward Dan. "For example, Dan might ask his potential client how much his services would be worth to the client if Dan won the case and the client was awarded $1 million dollars."

Scott pointed to the bracket approach on the board. "The third option—the bracket approach—usually works best when the prospect really has no idea what the investment should be. You might tell your client that you have a basic solution in the $12,000 to $18,000 range or a more sophisticated solution in the $32,000 to $46,000 range, and then ask which option is more in line with her budget. The solution you had in mind for her should be right in the middle of the first bracket. The larger number you mention likely will chase her back to the investment you originally had in mind."

Cheryl raised her pen. "So we want to remind the prospects about their problems and what those problems are costing them—in dollars and aggravation—before we throw out a number, right?" she asked.

"That's right," Scott responded. "It's hard to get a frightened kitten out of a tree. Try getting your prospect's attention back after you've scared him off with a big number without the proper setup."

Dan thought about Scott's three approaches but knew he'd have a hard time getting his prospective clients to be forthcoming about their budgets. Lawyers and money always put people on the defensive. "Scott, what if you can tell that your client really doesn't want to get into financials when you're meeting?" he asked.

"Good question, Dan. It isn't always easy to get prospects to open up about their budgets. A lot of times they say they're not sure. That's why the goal is to give the prospect an opportunity to estimate the problem's cost. If we can get them talking about the costs and then transition to the investment for a solution, there's a good chance they'll throw out a number that makes sense. And if you've done a good job of building perceived value in your service, the prospect may actually throw out a number far higher than your solution's cost, making it easier to close the deal when he finds out it won't cost him as much as he thought. This is also another place where the trust and likeability we've built are so important. Your prospects will be a lot more willing to open up to you about cost if you've established a solid relationship."

Dan nodded. He conceded that he needed to do a better job of financially qualifying his prospective clients. His scattered approach was probably wasting his own and his firm's time. Maybe Scott's strategies could help him target stronger prospects. He looked back to Scott.

"I'm a sports fan," Scott said. "And I have a baseball analogy for the sales process steps we've talked about over the past several weeks. I'm using baseball, but the idea applies to any sport or game where you have to follow established rules. Whether we're qualifying our prospect's pain, commitment, decision making ability or financials, we have to follow through on each of those areas. Baseball rules say that the batter must touch every base in order around the diamond. A player can't step up to bat, hit a single to center and run directly to second base. In addition to being out, you would end up on ESPN's dumbest plays of all time."

Scott was pleased to get a laugh out of his clients at his silly scenario.

He continued, "Anyway, just like the pro ball players, business development professionals can't skip steps either, such as going from the relationship-building step directly to the decision-maker step."

Scott drew a baseball diamond on the whiteboard.

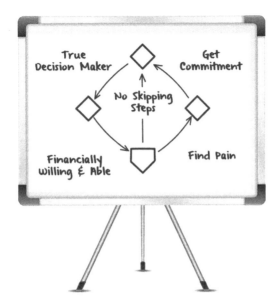

"So let's review the 'bases' we need to touch in order for us to round third base and get to home plate safely and score the run. Getting to first requires your ability to find enough pain, fear or perceived gain. Once you find those issues and repeat them back to your prospect, you're ready to run to second base. Arriving at second means you are now able to ask commitment questions. Once we know the prospect is a hundred percent committed to finding a solution to his issues and wanting our help to do so, we can safely move to third base," Scott said, pointing to third base on the board.

"Here, we acknowledge who else may be involved in making a high-impact decision and we identify what their process is for moving forward," he continued, drawing an arrow to home plate. "If everything lines up, we advance home to the financial step."

Cheryl caught Scott's attention. "What if everything doesn't line up? What if we get stuck on first?"

"Getting stuck on any of the bases will definitely happen at times," Scott said. "Let's say you're unable to move past first; you can't find any compelling reasons for the prospect to move forward with you. You have three choices: One, hold on first base until you find those reasons; two, determine that there aren't any reasons when you know that there should be, and question the prospect again, remembering to go deeper than those surface questions; and three, end the meeting and take the 'out' by moving the prospect to a 'no' outcome. Remember, being 'out' isn't always a bad thing. Sometimes it's a good learning experience, and sometimes it saves you a lot of time so you can focus on other prospects that are moving forward with you."

The important thing to understand is that touching each base allows you to further qualify your prospects. If you move into the commitment step without any reasons for them to commit, you'll get an out most of the time. Or, if your prospect is committed, but he's not the decision maker, you're likely not going to score. But if you follow the simple rule of not moving forward until you have successfully completed the previous step, you'll be in great shape to close a deal."

"That makes sense, Scott," Stacey said. "But how do I get the numbers if they just won't tell me?"

"It's true that some prospects will fight you every step of the way when you're trying to find out anything about their budget," Scott responded. "In that case, I suggest asking them about other similar projects. Try again to give them a range, and you should be able to at least get a feeling for whether they're going to be a financially viable prospect, even if they won't give you specific numbers."

Scott sensed it was time to wrap up.

"This week, try writing up scenarios where you'd use the direct, ROI and bracket approaches," he said. "Get used to how you'd proceed in a conversation based on what they tell you about their financials. Then, in your prospect meetings, try to include discussions about cost. When you're questioning your prospects, find out how much they'd be willing and able to pay for a solution to their problem. Now, time for our AHAs."

"I always dread broaching the money subject," Stacey said. "But today's discussion helps me see how important it is and gives me some tools to navigate the conversation and ensure I come in with the right numbers in my proposal."

"I agree," Cheryl said. "I've never framed the financial questions this way. Getting prospects to verbalize how much they'd be willing to pay to fix a bad situation is a great technique. And it will help me show what a valuable service I'm offering for a reasonable investment."

"Absolutely," Dan agreed. "This gives me a few different avenues to take to get my prospects to open up about their financials. If I give them a high and low range, for instance, they have to pick one, which will give me an indication of whether we're even on the same planet."

Scott nodded. "I want everyone to understand that this financial step is another critically important qualifier, just like the commitment and decision maker qualifiers. If for any reason your prospect isn't properly qualified for what you're offering, then you have to be prepared to move him to a 'no' and move on with more qualified prospects."

WEEK 9:
RATING THE PROSPECT'S COMMITMENT TO CLOSE

———

Scott's thoughts wandered to his clients again as he prepared the room for the next session. He always worried about his clients' ability to apply the strategies they'd discussed. Participating in a weekly training session was one thing, but translating the lessons from it into their own business development efforts was another.

That's why he always stayed in close contact with his clients. Being a sales coach didn't stop at the end of his classroom sessions. Scott routinely coached his clients for months on end—through late night phone calls, strategy discussions, meeting preparations and more—as they implemented his techniques to build their businesses. This group wasn't any different. Today, Scott was eager to present his pre-closing rating system technique to his clients.

At 8:00 on the dot, Stacey, Dan and Cheryl filed in, hands filled with coffee cups and notebooks. Scott smiled as they got settled.

"So, was everyone able to financially qualify their prospects last week?" he asked.

"I practiced the bracket approach, and I really liked it," Stacey shared. "It's really helpful for getting a sense of what ballpark your prospect is in."

"I agree," Dan said. "I asked one of my prospects about her current firm, the fees she was paying and whether she thought she was overpaying based on the firm's performance. I was able to find out that the rates she was paying were going to be pretty similar to my own, so the financial step wouldn't be a roadblock."

"I had a different experience," Cheryl said. "I was planning to present a $50,000 solution to a prospect, but in the financial step I uncovered that he was expecting something closer to $20,000. I was thankful to have found that out, and I was able to adjust my proposal to fit into his budget. I think I would have scared him off if I had come in higher."

"These are all really good experiences that you're sharing," Scott said. "Like I said, the more you practice, the faster you'll learn how to work through these steps naturally. Alright, we've covered a lot over the past few weeks, but there are a few more steps to the new sales process that we have to work through. Today we're going to be discussing a specific technique that may be used in order to test a qualified prospect's true interest and ability to moving forward to close. I mentioned this briefly when we talked through the commitment step, but I want to talk about it in more detail today."

Scott stepped back to the white board and wrote:

1-10

1. Define the "10"
2. Ask "why"
3. Identify what else is needed
4. Track your prospect to a "10"

"Whether you're rating a movie, a dining experience, or the pain level of a sprained ankle, you're likely to use a 1 to 10 rating scale. I want you to apply that same rating scale when you're judging what your prospects are thinking. Using the 1 to10 scale to quantify your prospect's commitment to move forward with you will help you get a much clearer picture of his true desire to solve the problems brought up during your meeting. Now, let me give you a few tips for using this technique effectively," he said, pointing to the board.

"First, define to yourself what your 10 is going to be. Is it a retainer, a next meeting or an opportunity to speak with the real decision maker? Because every situation may be different, it's important to *define* the 10 as it relates to that scenario. Once you've defined the 10, you're in a position to share that with your prospect and find out how close he is to meeting you at your pre-defined 10. So if your goal is a next meeting, simply ask him, on a scale of 1 to 10, where he sees himself as wanting to meet with you again. If he's a 6, 7, or 8, you're probably in a good position to move him forward to a 10. On the flip side, if he says he's a 2 or 3, it's a good idea to stop the sale and question why he is at such a low number. He may have met with you initially to fish for free information, and this technique can help you quickly uncover prospects that are just looking for free advice. Regardless of what it is, after you get the prospect's number, it's important to question him about why he chose it. Understanding his reasoning behind choosing that number can you give you great insight about where he is in the closing process. Then, take responsibility for that number. If you had truly qualified the prospect through the pain, commitment, decision maker and financial steps, the number likely would be high. If you skipped steps or didn't fully qualify the person, you're going to be hearing lower numbers."

Scott paused to let that point sink in. He knew salespeople never liked hearing that they were directly responsible for the prospect's disinterest. After all, it's always easier to blame other things when a deal falls through. But taking the time and effort to go through all of his steps would be the key to their success, just as he'd told them from the beginning of the class when he described how good behaviors, beliefs and attitudes would translate to results.

"Okay, once you understand why he's at that number on the 1 to10 scale, it's time to find out what he needs to see, hear or experience in order to move forward toward a 10.

Again, simply ask him what he needs to see, hear or experience to move your relationship forward. When you get the answer to that question, you'll have the information you need to track him to a 10."

Cheryl interrupted. "I'm not sure I'm clear on what you mean by track him to a 10. Could you give us an example?"

"Happy to, Cheryl. Let's say your prospect is an 8 and he says he needs to see pricing and understand how the solution works to fix her problem. That gives you the opportunity to bump him toward a 10 by saying something like: 'Outstanding. If I came back with a price that is in your budget and gets you the ROI you're looking for, and if the solution makes perfect sense, what would happen next?' He'll likely answer that he'd be ready to sign up. Or you could follow up by asking him directly if he'd be a 10 at that point. Whatever you do, don't miss the opportunity to finish the technique and try to get your prospective new client all the way to a 10. Otherwise, you're leaving the door open for him to drag out the sales process longer than it should last."

"Scott, I get the idea of tracking to a 10, but it sounds a little cheesy to me," Dan said. "I have to ask, does it really work?"

"Absolutely, Dan," Scott said, nodding emphatically. "This is one of the best techniques for getting a truly defined number that represents how prospects feel about potentially working with us. By using this technique, we can move them forward in a way that doesn't allow them to wiggle away from the truth. And this is where you'll hear the lies and truths come out. In sales, there's too much guessing involved and too many people living with false hope that they're going to get business. But with this 1 to 10 technique, you don't have to hope or guess. People will tell you what's going on. And if they don't, then that's a clear sign that you missed a step or you don't have a solid prospect in your hands."

Stacey raised her hand to comment. "It also seems like this is a good way to get the information you need to really customize the proposal to the prospect."

"Exactly," Scott replied. "This technique is so effective because by driving the prospect toward a 10, you're defining the next steps together. You're basically going through the proposal and the pains that need to be relieved, which sets you up to make a really strong presentation that will be specific to his needs. And that's where we'll leave today because next week we're going to talk more specifically about the presentation.

For your homework this week, think about your upcoming prospect meetings, and define what your10 is going to be for each one. Then think about how you're going to get your prospects to reach that 10. How about some AHAs, Dan?"

"I like this method. It seems like a concrete way to make sure you and your clients are on the same page. The prospect essentially creates the proposal for you."

"I agree," Cheryl said. "By tracking prospects to a 10, you're finding out exactly where they are and why, and what you need to deliver to get the deal. And it makes it hard for them to avoid moving forward."

"This is really going to help me tailor my proposal to their needs," Stacey added. "I can't believe I was trying to present my services in the first five minutes of every meeting before."

"These are fantastic AHAs," Scott said. "Remember, it's all about defining your expectation for the 10, then finding out where your prospective client ranks his interest in you, and then walking through what it would take to reach that 10. And I guarantee that this is a perfect way to lead in to your presentation."

WEEK 10:
THE PRESENTATION

Scott jumped into homework recaps at the start of the next session.

"Did anyone get the opportunity to use the 1 to 10 method last week?" he asked.

"I did," Stacey said, excited to share her story. "I don't know that I used it properly, but I did my best. I defined the 10 as moving forward with me and a 1 as having no interest in my plumbing supplies. The prospect said he was an 8, which I thought was encouraging. When I asked what else he needed to see or experience to move to a 10, I found out his decision would come down to whether my pricing was fair and in line with what he wanted to pay and how quickly his products would be delivered. So I asked him if he'd be ready to move forward if I came back with reasonable pricing and an acceptable delivery schedule, and he said he would. It was a really positive experience, and I think I would have fumbled my way through that conversation if I hadn't used the 1 to 10 method."

Scott smiled broadly. He loved hearing that his clients successfully applied his techniques. "I'm really happy to hear that, Stacey," he said. "I'm also happy to announce that today we'll be going over the final step of the sales process: the presentation," he said. "But I'm going to be talking about the presentation in different terms than you're probably used to. Most sales-people still think that closing a deal is all in the presentation—by pushing your features and benefits you persuade your prospect to buy. But I disagree. If you've properly implemented the process we've been discussing over the past several months, there should be very little pre-senting necessary in order to obtain the new business."

"Really?" Stacey asked. "That sounds too good be true."

"It is true," Scott said. "If you follow the steps we've spoken about and practiced, you'll start to see an amazing phenomenon—deals will actually close themselves. Effectively qualifying the prospect predetermines his movement forward to buy. Obviously you still have a presentation to make to discuss pricing or details to secure the engagement, but since the steps are defined so clearly, there isn't much to mess us up."

Scott looked over to Stacey . "Let's go back to the example we used last week where Stacey tracked her prospect to a 10. She found out that the prospect just needed to see pricing and delivery time. In fact, she told him that if she came back with a price in his budget and if the delivery time made sense, the next step would be signing the paperwork and getting started."

Scott looked around at his group. "So in this case, that means the presentation will only include the pricing and the delivery details specific to the prospect's needs—NOT everything Stacey's products have to offer. Business developers are notorious for presenting everything. Unfortunately, that strategy usually results in overselling, which turns the prospect off. So keep the presentation a hundred percent focused on what the prospect told you he needs to see, hear, or experience to close."

Scott quickly drew a grid on the board.

ISSUE	SOLUTION	100%

Check them off as you go

"Another important aspect to your presentation is clarifying that your prospect is a hundred percent in agreement as you walk him through your proposal. Start by asking, Does this make sense?' or 'Do you like the way this looks?' Then, to really hit home that you've nailed the solution and the prospect is happy, follow up by asking, 'A hundred percent?' On the other side of the coin, if there's a problem, stop and address it. The idea is to get your prospective new client to agree to everything and move the deal forward."

Scott paused and leaned forward. "My favorite closing line is, 'What would you like to do next?' The prospect's response to that question should always be a positive move forward toward the close."

Dan laughed. "You make it sound pretty easy."

"It can be—especially after you get used to the process and the steps start to flow naturally. The reason the presentation goes so smoothly is because of all the work you did to get it to that point," Scott said, making eye contact with each of his clients. "If you truly cover all the steps— all the way from the relationship to the spot-on presentation, the prospect becomes a client. And you know what else I want you to take away from this? If you struggled through the process or didn't get buy-in somewhere along the way, don't worry. By being genuine and friendly and asking questions, you're probably still ahead of 85 percent of your competition, because they likely didn't ask any questions at all. And remember the added benefit—you may get your prospect to a 'no' quickly and save yourself a lot of wasted time."

"Scott, is it okay to email our proposal to our prospects once we've gathered all the information we need?" Stacey asked.

"Stacey, I have to emphasize that you're going to want to go over your proposal face-to-face every chance you get. If it's a super-small proposal, I don't have a problem with an email. But anytime you're preparing a substantial proposal or you're working on an opportunity to get into an important target, the presentation of your proposal has to be done face to face. The only exception to that rule is if distance and timing don't allow to you do so, for example, if you just can't get on a plane to see the prospect. In that case, I recommend sending the proposal right before a scheduled call. That way you still have an opportunity to verbally walk through it point by point with the prospect, and you're there on the spot to answer any objections or questions that come up. And remember, by this point in the process, you should have the understanding in place that if the proposal covers the ground you previously discussed, then this prospective client will be turning into a new client."

Scott glanced at the clock as he wrapped up for the day. "And with that, we're back to AHA time."

"Don't over-present," Dan said.

Scott smiled. "Spot on. Short and sweet."

"That's my takeaway too," Stacey said. "I'm notorious for putting everything but the kitchen sink in my proposals. But with this method, I'll have already identified exactly what I need to be presenting."

"My takeaway is to walk my clients through each element of my proposal, either in person or at the very least over the phone. I need to make sure they are on board with each point as I go through the proposal, and that each point makes sense to them," Cheryl added.

"All very important lessons learned here," Scott said. "I hope you all can see how, taken together, all the steps involved in this process create a win-win situation. As you become an expert at using the process, the steps get easier and become more natural. The process just becomes a part of your efforts, and I guarantee you'll see better results. Alright, that does it for today. Next Monday, we'll put all these steps together and apply them in a mock sales meeting. Have a good weekend, and I'll see you next week."

WEEK 11:
PART 1 - THE ROLE PLAY

———

As he waited for Dan, Cheryl and Stacey on Monday morning, Scott hoped they had spent some time thinking about his process over the weekend. He knew they could succeed and overcome their challenges, but they needed to really commit to their business development efforts to achieve their desired results.

Stacey arrived a few minutes before 8:00 a.m., followed by Dan and Cheryl. As his clients settled in, Scott thought they looked bright-eyed for a Monday morning. It was the last day of the formal program, and he knew they were probably eager to wrap up and get back to their businesses. Hopefully, they'd be eager to implement everything they'd learned, too.

After chatting about their weekends for a few minutes, Scott got started.

"We've spent a lot of time over the previous weeks talking through the steps we need to execute in order to be successful in business development, but I've found that the best way to understand this process is to actually apply it. That's why I always end my workshops with a mock sales meeting. Before you all go off to implement your own business development efforts, I'd like to take some time today to show you how the steps from my process actually go together from start to finish. To make this even more realistic, I will be portraying the role of an attorney. As I go through the steps, take note of the language, tonality, and nurturing way that I deal with my prospect. Remember, we want to listen with our whole body and really 'be there' with the prospect. With experience and perfect practice, we don't have to think too much in order to move smoothly through our steps."

Scott started walking to the door. "Give me just a second to call in a colleague of mine who is going to help us today," he said.

"Alright, this is Jim, my vice president of operations," Scott said as he walked back into the conference room a moment later.

"Morning, everyone," Jim said as he walked past the conference room table. Scott led him to a smaller table set up at the front of the room.

"Jim's a great sport," Scott said as he and Jim sat down across from one another at the small table. "He's going to be my prospect in the mock sales meeting that we're going to run through this morning. Seeing this process play out from start to finish should really help solidify the steps in your minds. Please feel free to stop us if you have any questions or comments along the way. And I'll stop a few times to highlight some key points and ask questions as well."

Scott motioned to Jim. "For our purposes today, Jim is the CEO of a website development company, and I'm an attorney. This is our first meeting. Alright, let's begin," he said, turning to Jim.

"Hi Jim, it's nice to meet you. Thanks so much for coming in today. Did you have any trouble finding us?"

"No, not at all, my office is just down LaSalle. It was a nice walk up here," Jim responded.

"Great. Well, I know we were introduced through Fred Smith. How do you know Fred?"

"I play a lot of golf with Fred," Jim said. "He and I are old buddies and we have a membership together at a local golf club."

"Ah, safe to assume you've seen his left foot wedge?" Scott asked, laughing.

"I have." Jim smiled. "Fred speaks very highly of you, and yes, Fred does have a few tricks on the golf course, but he's a great guy."

Scott turned back to his clients. "As we talked about last week, it's helpful to develop a rapport at the beginning of the meeting. Be genuine about it, though. In this case, Jim and I have a friend and colleague in common. Remember, take the time to find commonalities and you'll build likeability and trust with prospects. And don't forget to set an agenda early on in the meeting."

Scott turned back to Jim.

"I appreciate you meeting me, Jim, and I want to make sure we make good use of your time, so if it's ok with you, I'd like to take a minute to set an agenda for today. Sound good?"

Jim nodded his approval.

"I know that we have about an hour, and from my perspective the purpose today is to see if there is a good *fit* for us to work together. I know you have some questions and issues, and I want to cover those. I'd also like to ask you some questions and try to understand what you're trying to accomplish with your business so I can see how I might be able to help. I just want to make sure that's okay?"

"Yeah, that's no problem," Jim replied.

"Sometimes I ask some tough questions. Being an attorney, I want to make sure I take a deeper dive and understand what's going on, so I want to make sure that's ok, too."

"Sure," Jim responded. "I'll give you whatever I can, and if you're going into territory I'm uncomfortable with, I'll let you know."

"Great," Scott said. "I'm curious to know, what are your expectations from our meeting today?"

"I just want to better understand your practice better and discuss a few issues I am having with my business." Jim stated.

"Perfect, Jim, we will be sure to cover that closer to the end of our meeting. To that point, by the end of our meeting today, we can expect to reach one of a couple outcomes. We may decide that we want to work on your issues together and you may be interested in retaining me as your attorney, in which case we can talk about next steps. Or, on the other hand, one or both of us might believe that we aren't the best fit for each other. If that's the case, I want you to know that it's okay to tell me that. I certainly won't hold any ill will toward you, and we can maintain a friendly relationship even if working together isn't a good fit. I'm not a perfect fit for everybody, and that's okay. Is that something you'd be alright with letting me know?" Scott asked.

"That's very nice of you," Jim said. "I appreciate you saying that, Scott. I prefer to be straight forward with people too."

Scott stood and turned his attention to his clients. "So you can see that I properly set the table, or the agenda for the meeting. I got the prospect to agree that we were meeting to see if there would be a good fit for my services. And I let him know that I wouldn't take it personally if he wanted to simply say 'no' at the end of our meeting—thus protecting myself from having to waste time later following up if he isn't interested. Is hearing this scenario play out helpful to everyone?"

"It definitely is for me," Cheryl said. "I can really hear the steps and detailed verbiage we talked about in your lectures."

Scott nodded. "That's great. Let's keep going. I'm going to move into the questioning step now with Jim."

He walked back to Jim's table. "So, Jim, I know we talked briefly on the phone, but tell me a little bit about some of the issues you've been recently facing with your business."

"Well, as you know, I run a website development company," Jim began. "We've been doing quite well and have branched into a lot of different services over the last few years. But as I mentioned to Fred, I have an issue that's driving me nuts. I keep losing my best salespeople. In the last three to five years, we've experienced a lot of unexpected turnover. Two of my best salespeople launched their own firms, and they're doing quite well. While I'm happy for them, there's also a maddening element to this, because they are using a lot of the skills, resources and tools developed here in their new businesses."

Scott nodded as he took notes. "So it sounds like you've had a number of talented people leave, and although you're happy for them, you're also worried about some competitive elements, in terms of those people using what they've learned with you to advance their own ventures."

"Exactly," Jim said. "My trade secrets are the lifeblood of my business, and I always fear that employees are going to take proprietary information and move on to greener pastures or use the knowledge they've learned here to build their own enterprises."

"That's certainly a valid concern. In addition to those issues, what else can you tell me about your frustrations, concerns or challenges?" Scott asked.

Jim sighed. "You know, I'm starting to ask myself if I really know how to keep my best salespeople. I'm concerned that I don't have the right elements in place in terms of contracts and employee packages. It seems like when my salespeople reach a certain level of success, they're easily lured away. This industry is still in a growth mode and there are a lot of small start-up companies looking for the best talent. My people are easy targets."

"I certainly understand that issue, and there are contractual items we can discuss, but I'll get back to those," Scott said. "Is there anything else you'd like to share with me? You've mentioned several issues already, but are there any other issues you're concerned about?"

Dan interjected. "It sounds like you're pressing him a bit, Scott. Are most of your prospects okay with that or do they start shutting down?"

Scott turned to the group. "Good question, Dan. Once you get people talking, they really start to open up. And as we talked about, it's really important to get a list of their concerns that you can work from for the rest of the meeting. Okay, let's hear Jim's response, and then I'll recap his frustrations."

"Every time I lose a salesperson it costs me a lot of money and time, which puts a strain on me and my business," Jim said.

"Let me recap some of your challenges," Scott said. "It sounds like we have three or four issues here. A lot of your salespeople achieve success at your company, but then go off to start their own ventures and end up competing with you. They're also taking some of your trade secrets and business strategies and using that information to drive their own businesses. There's also the issue of talented salespeople being lured away by recruiters because you don't have enough depth in your contracts and incentives to keep people long term. Then there are the replacement costs to you when you need to find new salespeople, which probably include paying your own recruiters and all the costs associated with hiring and training new people."

Scott paused to let the class absorb the list he'd developed in just a brief conversation with Jim.

"There are several challenging issues here, and I want to make sure we're focusing on the ones that are most pressing for you; the ones that you're losing sleep over, if that's the case. How would you prioritize these issues? "

Jim leaned back in his chair as he thought for a moment. "The more I think about these issues, the more I realize that I just can't afford to lose any more salespeople," he said. "It costs way too much to develop new talent."

"Alright, losing salespeople and the significant costs that go along with replacing them tops the list," Scott responded.

Jim continued, "Yes. Between recruiting fees, training costs and lost revenues, it costs well over a million dollars to bring in a new and experienced salesperson to replace one of my superstars."

"Those are definitely significant costs. How long has this been going on?" Scott asked.

"In the last five years, I've had seven or eight talented people leave suddenly. And these were people on whom I'd spent a great deal of time nurturing and developing," Jim said.

"And as you mentioned earlier, it probably costs well over a million dollars to bring in a new person to replace someone you've lost. I have to believe that the training and time you expend comprises part of that sum, but the bigger cost is probably the lost revenue when previously high-producing people are no longer generating new business."

"That's absolutely right," Jim agreed.

"So if we look at this, over the last five years, it may be as much as a $7 or $8 million problem. Would you say that's correct?" Scott asked.

"You know, I'd say it's at least over $5 million."

"When we think about that $5 million, if you continue to lose salespeople, theoretically you could be looking at those kinds of costs over the next five years. It could happen again and again, correct?"

"Yes, absolutely," Jim conceded. "So I need to talk to you about employment contracts, non-compete clauses and all that stuff."

"Of course," Scott said. "And that may be the tip of the iceberg. At this point, though, I want to understand the full impact of these issues on your business. We've discussed the financial side, but I also want to ask how this is affecting you on a personal level. In terms of your time and energy and how you feel about your company, what's going through your mind every time you lose a salesperson?"

"It's really infuriating me," Jim said, throwing up his hands. " I always get depressed when I know I have to bring in another new person and start all over. It really makes me want to give up trying to grow the business and just go back to selling on my own again."

Scott paused for a moment to address his clients. "What have I been identifying here?" he asked.

"Pain," Stacey said. "You've gotten him to talk about the financial and emotional impact on him and his business."

"Exactly right," he said, turning back to Jim. "Okay, this is all helpful for me to understand, Jim, and we have some compelling issues that we can work on in terms of losing salespeople. Let's also talk about the trade secrets issue. What do you think is the problem with your current non-compete agreement? Or, first of all, I should ask, do you have one?"

"I thought I did," Jim said, smiling wryly. "My current attorney worked it up about seven years ago. But I've found that it's not very enforceable. It's too fuzzy and broad in scope. That's the primary reason I wanted to talk to you today."

Scott nodded. "So that's the main thing that's keeping you from aggressively trying to prevent some of these former employees from competing with you?"

"I'd say so," Jim answered. "I'm not an attorney and didn't know there were holes in it. But as these guys have been leaving, I've learned that my current contract doesn't really have teeth to it."

"So one of the things we're going to have to get into is a much stronger contract to protect your interests moving forward. How would you say the trade secrets issue affects you financially?"

"That's harder to put a number on, but we've spent millions of dollars over the years developing new technology, and it would be disastrous for us to have information about that technology out there into competitors' hands."

"Right, and it sounds like that may already be happening to some extent, so time is of the essence to get some protections in place," Scott said.

"Absolutely," Jim replied. "Should we be stopping to discuss your fees now?"

"We definitely want to talk about my fees today, but that's probably step nine and I'm on step two here," Scott answered. "I want to make sure I fully wrap my head around what's going on and how I can help you make sure your success is yours and isn't helping other people in other ventures."

" I understand that, but I have to warn you that while I want to get this thing addressed, if your fees are going to run into the hundreds of thousands of dollars, it's probably not going to be a good fit for me."

"That's a different ballpark than what we'd be looking at in terms of trademarks and contracts and protections. Now if you decide you want to litigate, that's a different conversation and I can't make promises on that," Scott said with a smile. "Mainly I want to understand the issues that I can help you with immediately. When you mention trade secrets and the millions of dollars lost because of weak non-compete agreements that aren't protecting your interests, those are certainly things I work on. There are some significant issues here we should be able to take care of. It's just a matter of having the right person to help you; a person who has the experience to do it the right way," Scott explained, steering the conversation back to his next step.

"Please excuse me if this sounds like a crazy question," Scott continued, "but it's an important one for my understanding and for how we should look at taking next steps. When you talk about losing millions of dollars, the frustrations these issues cause you and the thoughts you mentioned about giving up the business—does all that add up to a 'should', a 'could', or 'must fix immediately' type of situation for you?"

"Oh, I have to fix this," Jim said. "It's imperative for me to look at some options for solving these problems."

"So would you say that this is something you'd like my help with if I presented you with some good solutions?"

"I would. I have to say I like the tone of the conversation so far."

"Alright, let's move into qualifying Jim as the decision maker," Scott said as an aside to his clients before turning his attention back to Jim.

"Jim, I know you're the CEO of your company, and you also mentioned having a CFO. In order to change attorneys and begin on possible remedies for your issues, is there anyone else other than yourself who would be involved in making the decision to change counsel?"

Jim thought for a moment. "You know, I'm going to drive the bus on this one. I have some advisors and key employees that have been with me for a long time, but this particular decision I will handle on my own."

Scott nodded. "I think that's wise. Some of your staff may have biased opinions if what we're putting in place negatively affects them, so it makes sense to keep this between us. How would you characterize your process for making this decision? Would you anticipate it being a fast process, where if we agree that we have good solutions for you, we'd get a retainer going right away and jump in? Or would you expect to be considering options for a while?"

"This is definitely on the front burner for me," Jim answered. "I may not be ready to sign something today, but it is something I want to get addressed, and I'm going to make a decision quickly."

"Alright, that sounds good. I know you voiced some concerns about my services running into hundreds of thousands of dollars. I want to ease your mind that the cost of my services, as they certainly wouldn't be that much unless we got into some pretty heavy litigation. Do you remember what you paid for your non-compete agreement and contracts seven years ago?"

Jim thought for a moment, "I believe it was around $10,000 or so if memory serves."

Scott looked Jim in the eye. "Based on what I'm hearing, we won't have a problem when we start discussing my fees," he said. "Once we examine all of your existing contracts and trademarks, , we will have a more specific idea of what range our fees will come in around. It might not be what you paid for your current protections, but when we look at where those have gotten you, obviously we want to put the best possible safeguards in place."

Jim nodded and leaned in. "On a side note, let me ask what you think, Scott. Can I go after these guys that left me?"

Cheryl laughed. "Sounds like he's looking for a little free consulting here."

Scott smiled at Cheryl. "He sure is, and I need to steer him back to my agenda."

Scott turned back to Jim. "At this point, I'd say you have to be careful about making decisions like that from an emotional perspective. There's probably some responsibility your company has to take for the mistakes that have been made. We'll certainly take a look at your current non-compete, and on the trademark side, we'll need to take a deeper look at your rights. As far as going after them for competing in the same market, based on what you're telling me about your current contract, we may encounter some trouble. Once I'm on retainer and get our priorities worked out, we'll be in a better position to look into options for litigation," Scott explained. "Just out of curiosity, is your current attorney handling a lot of things for you? Have you spoken to him about the problems with the non-compete provisions in their current form?" he asked.

"He's my general counsel, and he knows I'm not happy. However, he doesn't know I'm meeting with you today. He knows there needs to be some resolution to this, but to be honest, I'm not sure he has the ability to help me with these specific measures the way you can," Jim explained.

Scott smiled back to his clients. "See, we steered him back to the question at hand and got him to basically say that a change is inevitable. So let's see where he is on our 1 to10 scale."

"Jim," Scott began, "my firm is a full-service firm, so we can handle a number of different things. This said, I think for now, our focus should be on fixing mistakes that have been made in the past and learning from them rather than trying to change everything that's happened."

"I'm in agreement with that," Jim said. "If you end up thinking it makes sense to file a lawsuit, assuming you felt we had a high degree of likelihood I would get a good return on my investment; then I'd listen to options there, but I want to be level-headed on this and focus on fixing what we've discussed today."

Scott ran through what he and Jim had agreed on throughout the conversation.

"Okay, we've established that there are some problems here, and that there's a commitment to fix them. You're the person who will be making the decision, and we're not on different planets in terms of what the fees would be. So I think we're in really good shape. I don't have anything for you to sign today and would need to work up the retainer agreement if you did decide to work with me. My next question comes from getting to know you today and understanding what you're up against. On a scale of 1 to 10, with 10 being—'Scott, I believe that with your help we can turn this around in a short time and I'm very committed to working with you,' and a 1 being, 'Scott, I'm not interested in retaining you at this time and I'm going to live with these problems for now'—where would you say you fall as we're having this dialogue?"

Jim looked thoughtfully at Scott before answering. "Gosh, that's a good question and I see what you're getting at. I would say a 7 or 8."

"Good, those are positive numbers," Scott said. "I'm just curious, why 7 or 8? What prompted you to respond that way?"

"Well, for one thing, the referral from Fred was really strong. He's a trusted friend and business colleague and I put a lot of stock in what he has to say. Also, I like your style and the way you've handled this conversation today. I can tell you're not trying to force me into a corner. Your firm has a great reputation, and you have a great background. So I'd say all that adds up to the strong numbers."

"Thanks Jim. Obviously my job is to try to understand what your needs are, and part of doing that is to understand the gap between a 7 or

8 and a 10. I'd like to understand what you are looking to see, hear or experience beyond what we've covered today to feel a hundred percent comfortable in moving forward so we can start immediately addressing these issues."

"Even though Fred speaks highly of you, I'd love to see three or four validations from other clients you've worked with who have faced similar situations. Also, although this may be difficult at this point without having seen my contract, I'd like to see some type of proposed framework for the kind of work you're going to do for me that identifies what's first on the pecking order. I'd also like to see some kind of a plan that has your compensation attached to it. I have to admit that I haven't had great experiences with attorneys. It seems like when I've begun relationships with attorneys in the past, there hasn't been a solid understanding of what the time and fees were going to be. So I'd like to see an initial game plan with a strong idea of what I can expect to be paying."

Scott nodded and looked up from the notes he was taking to summarize Jim's points.

"With time constraints and confidentiality issues, providing three or four referrals may be a problem," Scott said, pushing back slightly. "You already know Fred, so what I'd like to do is offer up one additional referral in a similar industry. Between those two contacts, hopefully you can gain some good feedback about the services we provide. You'd also like to see a proposal that lays out a framework of the different things I'm going to be working on with you. We discussed the non-compete and trademarks and a few other legal issues that I'll include in that framework. I know how important it is for you to have fee expectations set, and I'll be happy to do that. I think you'll be fine with the range and structure I establish in the framework. We obviously can't predict if you're going to be interested in pursuing litigation, but you're aware that the deeper you get in to litigation, the more money is involved."

Jim laughed and agreed.

"Based on what we've discussed, it's really about putting together a plan, getting you some people to talk to, and making sure the framework is right. So let me ask: If that proposal is spot on or exceeds your expectations, where do you think you'd be on that 1 to 10 scale?"

"Well, I'd like to think I'd be all systems go," Jim said.

"A ten then?" Scott asked.

"Yes, a ten Scott." Jim replied.

"Fantastic, Jim. The next step is for you to send me your current non-compete agreement and trademarks to review. I'll review it, think further about what we outlined here today and put together a proposal. Let's set a specific time and date to meet next week. I think you'll be happy with what I bring back, and we'll be able to move forward together, ending some of these employment nightmares you've been experiencing."

"Thanks, Scott. That sounds wonderful," Jim said as he and Scott stood up to shake hands.

Scott paused to let the end of the role play sink in for his clients. "Alright, as you saw, Jim and I covered a lot of issues in that fairly short meeting, and I was able to lead him through each of the steps in our process. How did it sound and feel to you, Dan?"

Dan paused as he thought about how to phrase his response. "Well, I can tell you that I've certainly never had a meeting like that. Not to say that I haven't closed my share of business over the years, but mostly it was business that was highly referred to me. When I compare what I've been doing to what you just did, I have to say that I've been letting things go off course, answering too many questions and giving away too much free advice in my meetings. You dug deep and truly seemed to understand your prospective client. I really had some light bulbs popping off as I listened."

"That's fantastic, Dan. I know how different this process is for you, so I'm really impressed that you appreciated the flow of the meeting. Again, prescription before diagnosis is malpractice, right?"

Dan nodded in agreement.

"What are your thoughts, ladies?" Scott looked over at Stacey and Cheryl.

"Loved it! Can you do that again and pretend you are me," Stacey joked.

"What did you like or dislike about the role play, Stacey?" Scott asked,

"I enjoyed seeing all of the steps that you've been sharing with us the past few months being played out live in front of us. I was also impressed that you were able to play the role of an attorney, seeing as you aren't one. Or are you?"

"No Stacey, though I play one on TV," Scott teased. "I appreciate the compliment, but really it's a reflection of the third 'P' that we spoke about a while back. Remember performance improvement? I have been working and practicing this process for years," Scott added.

"How about you, Cheryl?"

"I enjoyed watching it as well. My concern is what to do when the prospect isn't following your script. And what I mean by that is when they try to ask questions or take back control."

"That's a great point, Cheryl. I know a role play can seem a bit staged. The truth is that most of your sales meetings will not go perfectly every time. Buyers will be difficult, ask price questions way too early and look for a competitive edge when they can. That being said, if you stay the course to the best of your ability, good things will happen for you. Think about it. The relationship established the rapport and trust from the beginning. The agenda set up the control element for us to keep on a win-win path throughout the meeting. I asked questions to uncover issues and pain, and I obtained commitment to fix the problems. Then, I properly qualified Jim as the decision maker and investigated his financial situation. At any point, I could have moved him to a 'no' answer or decided not to make a full presentation. Remember, even when the prospect doesn't stay on track with you, if the meeting is focused on him and his issues, you are going to come out in a positive light. You do the best you can to follow the process and that's all we can hope for."

"Think about an athlete who does his best and leaves everything on the field," Scott said. "Even if he loses, he knows he did everything to the best of his ability. This scenario is no different."

WEEK 11:
PART 2 -THE FINAL AHAS

———

Scott studied his clients before concluding his last class for them. Though he would be working with them individually over the next several months, they would not be coming back to class again. Scott had laid down the structure necessary for them to properly plan and execute a proven process to achieve results. Now it was up to them to take ownership of the process and make it happen. Scott often reminisced of the relationship between Michael Jordan and Phil Jackson from the Chicago Bulls franchise. Though Michael was a tremendously gifted athlete, he never really peaked until he had the opportunity to work with Phil. As the coach, Phil couldn't be on the court playing for Michael. He had to do his best from the sidelines, which is exactly where Scott found himself in relation to his clients. They had to play in the game, and he could only do his best to ensure they knew the right plays and had practiced perfectly.

"Alright everyone," Scott began. "We are rapidly coming to the end of our last session. I can't tell you how important it is for you all to continue your studies and to practice our processes every day. Even if it's just a small piece of the bigger picture, focus on it and get it internalized. I'd like to ask everyone to share their biggest AHA moments from the program. Cheryl, can you start?"

Cheryl thought about this for a few seconds before responding. "For me, the number one AHA has been the idea that it's okay to move someone to a 'no.' In fact, it's the second best thing I can hear from a prospect, because it will save me a lot of time, which is really important to me."

"Terrific. How about you Stacey?" Scott asked.

"I like the whole process because it allows me to gain and retain control over my prospects and the sales process itself. As you all know, I used to just walk into meetings and toss out information and proposals. Now I understand that it's all about asking questions and listening. If I uncover their key motivators, I'll know what to eventually present to them. The entire experience has been eye-opening for me. I really want to thank you, Scott"

"My pleasure Stacey. And the best way to thank me is to take your efforts to the next level. How about you, Dan? What was your greatest lesson learned?" Scott asked

"Well, I would say it's the idea that I am not really selling anything or anyone. The process is all about walking a buyer through a buying decision to see if there's a fit. I think I had been afraid of sales or even the concept of sales because of its negative connotations. I mean really, I hate salespeople as a general rule. Being an attorney, I never wanted to be seen that way. But now I recognize that I have the ability to understand my prospects' pains, fears or desires, and I can use that information to help them find the right solution. I think I've been hiding behind this idea that I'm not a salesman. You've shown me that sales is more about finding people who are qualified to work with me and highlighting how I can help them solve their problems. It becomes a win-win situation."

"Wow, you guys really exceeded my expectations on AHA moments. I really believe in you all and know that you'll find success in your business development efforts. Let's schedule our one-on-one meetings before you leave. Remember, I'll be here for you any time you have questions, and I'll be checking up on you to make sure you're following through on the steps. I want to thank you all for reaching out to me and for the time and energy you've invested in our class the past few months."

Scott smiled. "More good things to come."

EPILOGUE FROM THE AUTHOR

Thank you for reading my book. As you surely figured out some time ago, I am really 'Scott'; the principles he teaches throughout the story are the same ones I have the privilege of teaching my clients every day. I hope you found this distillation of my training program valuable. To allow you to better understand how far I've come, here is a little bit about my past.

My earliest memory of being an underachiever was in the 6th grade. Somehow I found myself in the principal's office with all of my teachers, my parents, and of course the principal surrounding me. The topic of the day: why was Steve Fretzin barely passing all of his classes? Maybe it was puberty kicking in or just a total lack of focus; I'm still not sure to this day. I remember my father asking me, "When are you going to get your act together and take your studies seriously." I'm pretty sure I told him I had the rest of my life to get serious or something like that, but that was my standard answer all the way through college. The unfortunate truth is that sometimes it takes a hard look at death to truly understand life.

When I suffered through the plane crash in 1996, everything changed for me. I wasn't going to allow my life to pass another day without making each one better than the last. In the years that followed, I took control of my life, and I took better care of my family, while working harder to improve my business life than I ever had before.

A few years later my life took another interesting turn; I met a sales coach. Though I had been through a number of training programs, seminars and had read most of the books on sales, nothing compared to having a coach. For the second time in a decade, I had the opportunity to dramatically alter my future. After six months of working with my coach I knew exactly what I was supposed to do with the rest of my life.

Being a sales coach has given me the opportunity to help thousands of people to improve their lives. I have never had more fun and felt such exuberance than working with my clients and watching them transform into selling machines.

My greatest hope is that this book helps you in your business development efforts. Though I strongly believe that selling excellence can't be learned exclusively from a book, you should now have many of the plans and processes necessary to radically change your approach to business development. It's time to let the traditional theories of sales go and rest in peace. Try to focus all of your energy on the prospective client's needs and desires. Think about it. No one ever got hurt by listening more and asking more relevant questions. Win or lose, make each experience an opportunity to improve and learn. In the end, you will find better clients that you will enjoy working with. Good luck and know that your dreams can come true if you work hard and follow a wiser path.

For more information on coaching services for you or your business, go to www.salesresultsinc.com

To download the documents mentioned in this book or to find out what happens to Dan, Stacey, and Cheryl, go to www.salesfreeselling.com.